GOLD RUSH
in the
KLONDIKE

JOSEPHINE KNOWLES

Gold Rush
in the Klondike

A Woman's Journey in 1898–99

Josephine Knowles

Fresno, California

Gold Rush in the Klondike
A Woman's Journey in 1898–99
by Josephine Knowles
Copyright © 2016 by Muriel James.

Published by Quill Driver Books
An imprint of Linden Publishing
2006 South Mary Street, Fresno, California 93721
(559) 233-6633 / (800) 345-4447
QuillDriverBooks.com
Quill Driver Books and Colophon are trademarks of Linden Publishing, Inc.
Book design by Maura J. Zimmer
Cover design by Jim Goold

Linden Publishing titles may be purchased in quantity at special discounts
for educational, business, or promotional use. To inquire about discount
pricing, please refer to the contact information below. For permission to use
any portion of this book for academic purposes, please contact the
Copyright Clearance Center at www.copyright.com.

ISBN: 978-1-61035-270-3
Printed in the United States of America
135798642

Library of Congress Cataloging-in-Publication Data on file

Contents

Introduction

Gold Rush in the Klondike: A Woman's Journey in 1898–99 is the true story of my grandmother's experiences as one of the few women among thousands of male prospectors who traveled to the Klondike in search of gold. Journeying with her husband, her 3-year-old son and a teenage nephew on boats, dogsleds and on foot, Josephine Knowles left behind the relative comforts of life in California for the snow and ice of Canada's Yukon Territory.

She and her husband crossed from Alaska, which was then a U.S. territory, to the Canadian mining town of Dawson, where she experienced the difficulties of survival in a rugged, inhospitable land. She witnessed the miners' hardships as men who had risked everything for gold descended into drunkenness and brutality, and as some were lost to starvation, typhoid fever and an ice-covered river near their cabin.

My grandfather, William Knowles, brought a load of shoes with them to sell to miners, and bought mining claims in hopes of bringing wealth back to their family in California. But like many others in the Klondike, my grandparents found a hard life subsisting on provisions including beans, applesauce and rations of bread, and weathering a winter that brought temperatures as low as 65 degrees below zero. The Klondike posed many

William E. Knowles was born in 1861 in Spencer, Iowa. He was a partner in the real estate firm Samuel & Knowles in Oakland. In 1897, he decided to travel to the Klondike and bought mining claims.

life-threatening dangers, but my Grandma's written account reveals that through it all, she was courageous and compassionate, and also curious about the people they met and the vast wilderness that surrounded them.

When I was a little girl, I loved to listen to the stories she would tell our family, especially on Thanksgiving, when she often shared memories of the gold rush. With earnings from real estate and their investments in the Klondike, my grandparents had returned to California and built a house in Berkeley. Sometimes, I sat on the floor behind the sofa at the house while my grandmother interviewed college students who were interested in renting a room. She would often ask them, "And what else interests you here at the university?"

I remember asking her why she would pose that question so often, and she replied: "That's the way I keep up on my education." My Grandma, whom I called "Mema," was deeply inquisitive and constantly interested in learning about new subjects. Years later, I saw that quality captured in her notes about the Klondike Gold Rush.

When she was sick and bedridden near the end of her life, she handed me a small wooden box filled with pieces of paper. They included her writings about the gold rush.

"Muriel, do you think these are worth being published? Look them over and see what you think," she said. She asked if I could edit her book, and perhaps get it published.

For many years, her manuscript remained in a box, and unfortunately I misplaced it. But some years ago, I found the box in my messy garage, and I became fascinated with the story she told.

The manuscript was typed and held together with paper fasteners. The title page[1] read "The Klondyke in '98: By A Woman Who Was There." The typed pages included corrections where words had been blotted out with X's and revisions had been made in pen and pencil.

In editing my grandmother's writings, I have tried to leave her words largely untouched and have edited the text sparingly, mostly to repair fragmented sentences, insert necessary background,

---

1. The title page says Josephine Knowles' manuscript was "Transcribed and Organized from Original Notes by Robert Tryon." There is no reference to the year in which it was typed.

Josephine Knowles in the early 1900s. She was 34 when she left San Francisco bound for the Klondike in 1898, and she later wrote about her experiences during the gold rush.

or fix small grammatical mistakes. I have changed the names of some chapters.

My grandmother's story begins with her memories of an emotional conversation with her husband, who wanted to join the gold rush but was distraught about leaving his family behind. He soon traveled to the Klondike alone but was unsuccessful and lonesome, and returned to California. He then made a second trip to Dawson, and when he returned home was convinced he would need to stay in the Klondike for a full year. He asked Josephine to return with him and bring along their young son, and she agreed.

Recalling her emotions at the time, she explained that her family had struggled financially since they moved away from their farm in Nebraska to the town of Selma in California's Central Valley. Her father, Jay N. Skelton, was a physician and schoolteacher, but she said that in California life had not been easy in Selma or in Oakland. Given the opportunity to go to a place where people were finding gold, my grandmother said she thought: Why not?

They traveled by steamship to Seattle, where they bought a year's supply of food, and then sailed on toward Dyea, Alaska, near the Canadian border and the Klondike.

Those they met on the journey included the young writer Jack London, who traveled on the same boat with them and lived nearby once they had reached Dawson. My grandmother said Will was friendly with the author, who had told him of smuggling a supply of whiskey inside pickle barrels to avoid paying duties on the liquor. She shared her impressions of London, saying that although he was a great writer, he had a "haughty and superior air" toward others and had moved his camp after arguing with neighbors. She said she had a negative impression of the writer most of all because he beat his dogs, remembering that one night she heard him drunkenly cursing and striking the animals as they whimpered in pain.

She also fondly recalled the generosity of people like Clarence Berry, a businessman who was also from Selma and who made a fortune in the gold rush. When she was seriously ill, Mr. Berry had fresh milk brought to her from his cow, and she insisted that cow had ultimately saved her life.

During her yearlong stay, she met Native American men and women, and visited an Indian burial ground filled with totem poles. She once described the colorful scene in a saloon, peering down from the second floor on a room filled with gambling miners. She marveled at the beauty of the mountain landscapes, and of the colors of the Northern Lights.

Observant and thoughtful about her experiences, she told the story of her year in the Klondike with intelligence and enthusiasm, and provided a vivid account of life during the gold rush.

—*Muriel James*

A Note to Readers

Gold Rush in the Klondike was written in the early twentieth century about events of the year 1898–1899. Josephine Knowles' account of her adventures in the Klondike is presented here as she wrote it, in her own language. Some of the terms Knowles uses may be offensive to modern readers; nonetheless, the editors have chosen to present Knowles' complete and unexpurgated text in order to maintain the accuracy of this contribution to the historical record.

CHAPTER I

Our Search for Gold Begins

Ishall never forget a certain night in the year 1897. My husband, William Knowles, had come home from his office looking tired and worn. As he sat by the fire with our little son on his knee, trying to keep the child quiet until dinner was ready, he visibly appeared to be discouraged and downhearted. I could see that something was bothering him, but I thought it best not to ask questions.

After dinner he romped with the children for some time, but when Hazel, our second daughter, played several pieces of music for him on the piano, I could see tears on his cheek. While I put the children to bed and finished my work in the kitchen, I was somewhat troubled by the careworn appearance of my husband. My lot in life had not been an easy one, for I had gone through many hardships in coming from Nebraska to Selma, California, and even Death had once entered our door and taken away one of my little ones. And now, the demeanor of my husband gave me the impression that something terrible was hanging over our home.

I went into the parlor where the fire was burning brightly, and made things look home-like and comfortable. Will stood by the fireplace looking at the blaze, which cast a mellow glow about the room. I went to him, and putting my hand on his shoulder, said quietly, "Will, what is the matter? What is troubling you?"

He put his arm around me and led me to the sofa, where we sat for a few minutes without saying a word. At last he got up and walked several times around the room. Then, leaning against the mantle piece, he sighed as he turned to me.

Stopping to lean against the mantle piece, he sighed as he turned to me.

"Joe," he said, using the diminutive of my name, "if it were not for you and the children I could go to Dawson, where I could make some good money. It makes me very discouraged to see all my friends going to Alaska while I am tied down. Here in Oakland, I have been trying so hard to make a start, but everything seems to be against me." Then after a pause he added, "Mr. Samuel told me this morning he would 'stake' me financially if I would go to the gold country!"

I looked at him in amazement. Will had not said a word of the Klondike before, and until now had seemed despondent over his work. Despite many reverses he had always had a contented and hopeful nature. Five years before, we had lost everything we owned and moved from Selma to Oakland, thinking to make a new start in life. My husband became acquainted with a man by the name of Samuel, who had taken him as a partner in the real estate business, in which my husband had some previous experience.

I could see that Will was very serious, and realizing the significance of what he was thinking, I began to tremble, my knees shook, and for a minute I thought I might faint. But in a moment, I had myself in hand and had made up my mind about what to do. Stepping over to where he was standing, I said firmly: "Will, when does the next boat start for Dawson? Tell me what must be done first to get you ready for your trip."

"Joe, you know that I could not go and leave you alone with the children. I might not get back for a year or two. And another thing, I haven't money enough to keep you comfortable while I am away. How could I manage it?"

Then we began to plan, and it was almost morning before we had worked out a feasible program that would make his trip possible. I would go with the children to live with my mother in Selma while he was gone. After buying him a year's outfit for the Alaskan trip, I would have fifteen dollars a month to live on; but we figured that we could manage some way. At any rate, here was a chance for a new start in life and we were willing to stand the necessary privations that would result. But despite these plans my husband was not decided, and he went to bed very much troubled.

The next morning we said nothing of our plans because we did not want to mention the subject before the children. After Will went to work, I took the curtains down and began to pack some things. When he came in for lunch he saw what I had done, and said in a surprised voice, "Joe, why have you taken down the curtains?"

And then, as he suddenly realized the significance of the packing, he cried, "Put them up again!"

I went over to him.

"Will, you are going to Dawson. You might just as well give in, for you *are* going!"

I saw a change come over his face. He sank into a chair by the table and put his head in his hands. Then in a moment he looked up at me and said shakily, "Joe, I will go and God bless you, Joe—my Joe!" And he jumped up and went out the door, forgetting all about his lunch.

It was now Wednesday, and there were only three days to prepare him for his trip. The boat would sail on Saturday. As I hurriedly packed all the necessities, the tears sprinkled everything, and I felt that the very bottom of my life had fallen out. Will had so many things to attend to in getting ready that he did not notice how weary and badly I felt. In the rush of preparing his outfit and settling business affairs, time passed swiftly, and Saturday came altogether too soon.

It was only through the influence of friends that my husband was able to obtain passage to Alaska on "The Bear." This boat was crowded to the utmost every trip it made. At times men actually fought for a chance to go on her. In many respects, the trip was unpleasant. There were no accommodations whatsoever, as the boats going to Dawson were very small. Only the lucky found places to sleep.

My husband took enough food and clothing to last him one year. It is easy to imagine how cumbersome was his outfit, which consisted mainly of dried potatoes, beans, bacon, eggs and butter put up in cans.

By Friday night, everything was ready for the long journey. That morning I had killed chickens and had made some goodies for the trip. This proved to be fortunate, for the food along the way was atrocious, and my basket was like caviar among swine.

The thought of our parting, and the fear that my husband might back out at any moment, made the night sleepless for me. As for my husband, several times during the night he went into the children's room, stood and looked at them, and then went back to bed without saying a word.

I accompanied my husband to the Oakland Mole[2] the next morning. On account of the children, I did not go across the bay to San Francisco, where my husband was to take his boat. Our parting was simple but very painful to me. The last kiss, the waving and shouting of good-bye of the children, a few tears and he was gone.

My husband's trip was very hard on him. He changed boats at Seattle, for he planned to make his way to Dawson by "packing" over the Chilkoot Pass. The overloaded boats landed near Scagway at Dyea, and from there travel was overland to Dawson, by means of wagons, dog teams and sleds, or by ordinary "hoofing it." It was necessary to go into Dawson early in the spring before the Yukon River broke up. It was also easier to pack over the mountains when the snow was on the ground.

This journey was very difficult, as it was necessary for him to "pack" his supplies from Dyea to Sheep Camp, and from there over the lofty Chilkoot Pass to Lake Lindeman. Near the top of the pass was Crater Lake, where he made a temporary camp near the water's edge. He spent three weeks carrying his supplies from Sheep Camp to this place, and another week transferring his supplies to Lake Lindeman. As the Indians asked exorbitant prices for packing equipment for the miners, it was necessary that my husband do it himself.

---

2. The Oakland Mole was another name for the Oakland Long Wharf, where ferries departed for San Francisco.

Later he told me that when he put his last pack down on the ground at Lake Lindeman, so exhausted was he that his nose began to bleed profusely. His feet were so swollen that he could hardly step on them, and he had to tie gunnysacks around his shoes to keep the rocks from piercing through the soles. All the first night at the lake, he suffered the agony of exhaustion accentuated by discouragement. He could do no work the next day because of the tender condition of his feet.

At this point he cut timber and made a boat with which to proceed down the lake and river to Dawson. As he was not strong and unused to the dangers and privations he met along the way, at times he would almost give up in fear and discouragement.

He finally arrived in Dawson in June, when the weather was warm and the snow almost gone. For quite a little time, he looked around and studied the mining situation, staking several claims for himself. But it took only a few weeks for him to realize that he had made a great mistake. He found that he did not know the first principles of mining and that he did not have the endurance to stand the hard work of a miner, and he soon concluded that he would return home at the first opportunity.

It occurred to him that he might be able to make a good deal of money on the "Outside"[3] by forming corporations and stock companies for the purpose of financing mining exploitations in the Yukon. With this thought in mind, one November day in Dawson, when the temperature was so far below zero that the cold was almost unendurable, he decided that he would not remain there any longer. Homesick and longing to see his family, he hired an

---

3. This term was often used to refer to the world back home, outside the Klondike.

Klondikers with supplies at the Scales, preparing to ascend to the summit of Chilkoot Pass in March 1898.

Indian guide and dog team out of the few funds he had left, and started for the "Outside."[4]

As I was sitting with my mother one Sunday, my eyes fell on a newspaper article that gave me a delightful shock. It told of the quickest trip ever made out of Dawson, made by W.E. Knowles— my husband! He had arrived the night before and was on his way to join his family. One can readily imagine our excitement when we read this news, for we had not expected him home for a whole year.

---

4. According to an article in the *Oakland Tribune* published after his return in December 1897, he bought a mining claim in partnership with Frank Berry for $250,000 and claimed "to have made a rich strike." See Appendix.

At six o'clock he arrived, making the most impressive appearance. As he had no other clothing, he was dressed in furs from head to foot. But his face showed the innumerable hardships that he had suffered; he looked emaciated and sick, having lost a great deal of weight on this terrible trip.

Yet we were a delighted family that greeted him. We knew that there were many other homes that had sent some of their men out on this precarious journey and had never got them back again. But our joy at his return was not permanent, for the next May my husband decided to brave again the same hardships by going to Dawson on a short business trip. He was much more fortunate this time, and returned home in three months.

At breakfast the morning after his return, while we were talking about the children and all the things that had happened while he was away, I saw that he was disturbed. Suddenly he reached over and took my hand.

"Joe," he ventured, "I came out this time to get you. I found out that I will have to stay in Dawson a year or I will lose everything that I have invested. But I cannot stay away from you and the children for so long again. Do you think it possible for you to go back with me?"

At first I did not know what to do or say at my husband's sudden proposal. I merely sat looking from him to the children and back again. Then, I became excited thinking of our possibilities.

"Will, do you really mean it? I have been hoping all along that it might be possible to go with you and that you could find some way of taking me along!" He smiled, and I almost wept in my delight.

CHAPTER 2

Off to the Yukon

Soon we had made all the necessary arrangements for the trip, and our preparations were very hurried in the short time we had before we were to sail. It was decided to leave my two little girls with my husband's sister in the Santa Cruz mountains, and we were to take her oldest son, Charlie, along with us. As for my little three-year-old son, Willie, of course I would have him with me, despite all the hardships we would probably face. I made the baby, as we still called Willie, some warm clothes, and also some for myself. I knew we would have to have furs later in the season, but these we could buy in Seattle, where we would stop off several days on our way to Dawson.

Leaving my daughters, Rose and Hazel, was difficult, but they did not seem to feel badly when I saw them off to their aunt's. They seemed to look forward to their visit with delight, for their aunt had a large family and they would be happy and contented with their cousins. They took the train with their father, and we said goodbye at the train station.

The steamer Queen *about to depart Seattle for Alaska on March 6, 1898. Some of the people crowded on the pier are sitting on wooden crates of lamp oil. During the spring and summer of 1898, steamers were filled with people traveling from Seattle to Alaska on their way to the Klondike.*

By the next Saturday morning we were ready for the boat. When little Willie, as we sometimes called him to distinguish him from Will, his father, saw the boat we would be taking, he fell all over himself in excitement. And he was so healthy and strong, and such a good sport, that I knew he would give us very little trouble on the trip.

Our voyage to Seattle was a stormy one. Almost everybody on board the steamship was quite sick. The captain was very kind, and brought two small barrels into the salon for the children to play with. There was one other married woman aboard, with a little boy about Willie's age, and the two had a lot of fun together.

Arriving in Seattle, we bought a whole year's supply of food, and also some clothing. We made definitive plans for our journey over the mountains to the Yukon River. My husband felt it impossible for him to carry our outfit over the Chilkoot Pass as he had done before, so we were much relieved and pleased when we found that Indians could be hired to pack our goods very reasonably at this time of year.

At last everything was packed and ready, and as we sailed out of Seattle bound for Dyea, Alaska, for the first time I began to feel the reality of going to a land "far, far away" from civilization, where everything is cold and desolate, and where one does not see the sun eight months of the year.

At times I almost wished that I would get a telegram telling us that our two girls were ill, and that we must turn back. But as nothing of the kind happened, and as day-by-day we approached Alaska, I made a resolution to be brave in every situation and never to complain. This determination, which soon became a conviction, helped me in many ways later while in the North.

In going to Dyea we had to pass through some very dangerous waters among the innumerable islands that dot the lower Alaskan coast. We took on an Indian pilot, who steered us instinctively over the many treacherous shoals. At one place we went through "The Narrows" where, I remember so vividly, there were fearful, swirling whirlpools, and where we made sudden, frightening turns. At any moment we all felt as if the boat were going to be dashed on the rocks, and then suddenly we would find ourselves in smooth waters.

Supplies are loaded onto a steamer in Skagway harbor, Alaska, in 1897.

We briefly stopped at various places on our way: at the Treadwell mines for a few hours, where the people of the town showed every kindness in making our stay pleasant, for they knew that we soon would be cut off from all communication with the outside world; and at Skagway, where we found an old Indian burying ground. The burial place was fascinating because of the many grotesque totem poles that marked the graves of the Chiefs. These monuments, which rose up into the air twenty feet, were covered with carvings of great ugly snakes, toads and other gruesome creatures. Leaving here after a few hours stop, we soon landed at Dyea, where we were to bid farewell to all connection with the world, the "Outside," and from where our harrowing journey over the mountains to the Upper Yukon was to begin.

FRANK H. NOWELL, ALASKA STATE LIBRARY (P48-150).

Teams of horses and people on the dirt street in Skagway, Alaska, on May 20, 1898.

The wharf at which we landed was the scene of many brawls, where ugly and bad natures began to expose themselves. As we were now entering English territory, the custom officers were rummaging through the various outfits looking for whiskey and tobacco, on which there was heavy duty. Everything was confusion, because all the outfits had been thrown into the bottom of the boats without order or system. Every man had to find his own equipment, parts of which he sometimes found in somebody else's hands. The men were serious, and meant business, for nothing could be bought in the tiny town of Dyea and the loss of an outfit meant having to return to the States. Those who could not find their things were

Storefronts in Dyea, Alaska, circa 1898.

not allowed to go on. My husband stood beside me, and said in a low voice, "Joe, either keep perfectly quiet and say nothing, or go immediately ashore. These men stop at nothing here, after going through so much to get this far. If you want to watch, stay perfectly still."

Some of the things I saw were strange and horrible to me, for I was not used to seeing and hearing such low conduct. Men were swearing fearfully, and squabbling over trifles. Occasionally I saw a terrible fistfight. Yet, disgusting as it was, I could not help but pity these men. Each man had brought only enough to carry him through the year, and those who could not find their belongings had to go back on the next steamer. We managed to collect our things without much trouble, and after looking them over several times, gave away what we could do without.

On the Yukon Trail in the Dyea Valley, Alaska, 1898. In Winter and Pond Company's photograph album "The Trail of '98."

During the tension and excitement, my husband suddenly nudged me, and whispered: "See those 'pickle' barrels over there? They are part of the outfit of Jack London."

Though there was nothing unusual about the appearance of the barrels, I was told that in the middle of each barrel was a goodly quantity of whiskey, which in this way happily escaped duty.

After all of these years, I feel that I can now tell the truth about my experience, especially when I feel that the truth will not now hurt anyone. We all know of the unfortunate career of Jack London, and of his misfortunes, and perhaps my own impression of him can contribute a little to understanding of his life and character.

Great writer though he was, my own feelings toward him as an individual were negative. He came from Seattle on the same boat with us, and we saw him frequently on the trip in, as well as in Dawson. He and my husband became friendly, and thus it was that

"Favorite dog team of Sheep Camp," circa 1898. Men and dogs in front of the Mascot—where a sign read "Hot drinks, meals, lunches, and beds"—and other buildings along the trail.

he imparted to my husband the secret of the pickle barrels. I shall have more to say about him in later pages.

Realizing that the real work of the trip was before us, we rested several days at Dyea. Before us stood the mountains, about ten miles distant, and our worst journey would be over the Chilkoot Pass to the lakes beyond. My husband managed to hire a whole Indian family to carry our outfit over the Pass, the boys carrying about seventy-five pounds, and the men, two hundred. We started out early in the morning for Sheep Camp, at the foot of the Pass, and it was an interesting sight to see our Indians heavily laden but jogging along in single file.

Sheep Camp in April 1898. Tents and buildings line the trail through Sheep Camp en route to Chilkoot Pass.

Instead of having to hike, I traveled to Sheep Camp in luxury, riding on an old wagon with a rough board for a seat. There was no road—there were no roads to speak of in Alaska then—and we bumped and jolted for hours over boulders and rocks, and more boulders and rocks. At times it was necessary for the men to get out and move some of the rocks aside to let the wagon through. To stay in the wagon meant holding on for life, but we managed to pass the time with interrupted conversation. On the way we passed a number of small creeks that were filled with fish. So numerous were the salmon that the men found great sport in trying to catch them. Our Indian dog continually jumped into the water, caught a big salmon, shook the fish until it was dead, and then, carrying it to us in the wagon, would go back for another.

Once during the day, we felt a rumble of the earth, but at the time thought nothing of it. Later we discovered that the sound had been of a glacier that had crashed down on Dyea, killing many men and doing considerable damage. The very hotel at which we had stopped had been completely obliterated. That morning when we had left, I had by chance noticed the glacier, which though it looked very close, still was three miles away. It looked threatening, and as if that whole body of ice might come down at any moment, and I had actually spoken of it. We could not help but feel now that Providence had saved us from a calamity.

I was totally exhausted when we reached Sheep Camp at about six o'clock that evening. We were all hungry and anxious to find some place to rest our weary bodies. As we stopped before the door of a place called a "hotel," I saw that it was a mean hovel in which we were to spend the night. When I descended from the wagon and landed on my feet, down I went to the ground. I was stiff and sore and could hardly stand, but I managed to walk into the hotel with difficulty. Supper was ready, and we sank down on the crude benches at the table. Our fare consisted of beans, ham and eggs, sourdough bread and coffee. But I think that I never tasted a better meal.

Our "hotel" consisted of two rooms and a big attic. When we arrived, the place seemed already crammed and running over with guests, but the proprietor greeted our party of twenty with a smile and a promise of accommodations, though I could not see how or where we were to sleep.

While I was sitting at the table, I had a chance to study the men who were eating their supper. Most of them were in their thirties, and quite a few were much younger. This was my first meeting with mining men, and I was surprised to note the appearance of refinement and of good breeding in most of them. They were all talking about some new and rich "strike" in Dawson. This spectacle was of course absorbingly interesting and exciting to me: these roughly dressed men enthusiastically talking "gold" while the flickering candles, which almost went out at times, cast dancing shadows over their features, and the sounds of talking and the occasional chorus of laughter at jokes suddenly "sprung." While listening to their laughing and joking, I wondered at the apparent joyousness of these men who were suffering so many hardships.

And then I began to realize that after all it does not matter whether in the city, on the sea, in the mountains, or in the little log cabin by the famous Chilkoot Pass, men can always be happy by just being "good sports." I remember that as I was sitting there, one man began to find fault with others and make unpleasant remarks about them, and was suddenly told to "Mush On." This means "go" in the North, and the complaining fellow left immediately.

This particular hotel had housed thousands of men going into the North. If these old logs could have told stories, what a fascinating book would have been written! Many a man had started from here with a heavy pack on his back trying to get over the Pass—which is very precipitous and rocky, without any definite trails—and many had never made it, becoming sick or discouraged by the grueling task. It took about three weeks of continuous travelling back and forth for a single man to carry his year's supplies from Sheep Camp

ERIC A. HEGG. ALASKA STATE LIBRARY (P124-04).

Prospectors with piles of supplies at the Scales, located at the base of Chilkoot Pass, in 1898. In the background, a line of people climb up the snow-packed trail headed for the summit.

to Lake Lindeman, which is over the pass and in the headwaters of the Yukon. Many had lost their lives through freezing when sudden storms arose.

After supper our job was to find a place to sleep. The next day would be our worst, for we had to go over the Pass, which now lay right in front of us. In the rear of the room we saw a wooden stairway leading to the loft, and with Willie in his arms, my husband went up. Soon he came down and told me that he had found a place in the far corner of the attic for us to sleep. Charlie, our nephew, had to stay downstairs and find a place on the floor somewhere.

On entering the attic, I was taken aback by the sight of the tired men lying like animals all over the floor, trying to find sleep on those hard rough boards. They had no pillows or blankets. The floor itself had huge cracks in it, through which one could see the flickering light below. On one side was a rough bunk where a man and his wife lay sleeping. By the dim light of a candle, held in place by three nails driven into a box, I could scarcely see where to step over the forms of the men so as to get to our sleeping place. Our bed consisted of a fur robe thrown on the floor, and that was all!

This was only the beginning of a series of hard beds I was to sleep on, for whereas this bed was merely hard, many times after I had to sleep outdoors on earth that was bumpy and full of rocks. All that night the men moaned, while a few snored loudly. It was little wonder that they groaned, for all day they had been packing a hundred pounds of food, and few of them had muscles trained for such a burden. I could sympathize with their fatigue; I felt the same. Yet a sense of wonder so possessed me that it was almost morning before I dropped off to sleep.

The breakfast gong was a welcome sound the next morning. All night long the odor of ham and eggs had come up to us, and with the rattling of dishes and the howling of dogs, sleep was out of the question. Early as it was, when we went down to the table, everyone was there. There was a candle at both ends of the table, and we all looked like ghosts in the dim light. The breakfast was soon over and we made preparations to leave.

At 6 o'clock we departed from Sheep Camp, amid cheerful good-byes and hearty handshakes with the ones that we left behind. We were now at the very base of the mountain, and it was a long way up the Chilkoot Pass to the summit, which we had to climb that day. The early morning air was clear and so cold that we were compelled to walk fast to keep warm. My husband was also anxious to get over the Pass and to on Lake Lindeman before night, so we hiked and climbed using all our energy all day.

There was potential danger of being caught in a storm on this trip, and such a mishap might have been disastrous. The semblance of a trail was very rocky and steep, so that we had to crawl on hands and knees at times. Little Willie walked a good deal of the way, and considered it quite a lark. Everyone on the trail, homesick for little children, enjoyed his company very much, and several men carried him for short distances.

Thus we trudged up and up until I became nearly sick with fatigue. This body-breaking climb was especially hard on horses that people had atrociously overloaded. Many horses had died from exhaustion on the very path, and occasionally we came to a corrupted carcass from which arose such a horrible stench that it made me very ill. At about three o'clock in the afternoon, I felt that I could go no farther, and as everything began to get black before my eyes, my husband came to my rescue and guided me to a rock where I sank down. In a kind of stupor I looked down far below, and it seemed impossible that I had walked up this distance.

Feeling groggy, I looked about me and became almost dizzy with the sight of the immense valley, lined with mountains that seemed to touch the very sky. As I gazed about, the awe of it all, my fatigue, and the bad odor of decaying flesh rather overcame me, and all at once I tumbled off the rock in a faint. Luckily my husband had found a tent nearby, where he carried me and laid me on a camp bed. Though the blankets were in rags, and had apparently never been aired or washed, I fully enjoyed this soft bed, especially as I felt very tired and sick.

The Indian who owned the tent brought me some hot coffee in a pot that had never been washed, and opened up a can of pears. Though this repast and respite cost us five dollars, I felt very lucky and thankful for the hot drink and fruit juice. An Englishman brought some whiskey, which he offered to pour down my throat, but I refused it. There were others around, however, who gladly accepted his offer. Soon I was revived and we started up again.

It was a terrible climb all afternoon, over rocks and boulders, with the summit getting nearer and nearer, yet still so far away. We had to fight every minute, and at times I thought I was losing. My husband and nephew took turns carrying Willie, pushing him up over boulders, then climbing up after him. The poor little fellow got very tired, being pushed and jerked about. He and the son of the other married woman in the crowd would occasionally look at each other and laughingly throw sticks and stones for the little Indian dog, Pete, who at first would scramble after them but later became so exhausted from his playful endeavors that he hardly reached the summit.

At six o'clock we reached the summit, and though tired and worn out, were almost transfixed by the wonderful scenery around us. The air was clear, with not a cloud to mar the beauty of the mountains that surrounded us. Though winter had not yet come, we could see snow capping several peaks, and glaciers and crystal rivers running through the numerous valleys. The reflection from the setting sun tinted everything with marvelous colors, and at every turn of my head, I would see new beauties. Looking down from the other side of the summit, right at our feet was a small, clear blue lake, called Crater Lake. It is at this lake, which is several miles long, that the great Yukon River has its beginning, flowing to the north-east through Lake Lindeman, then Lake Bennett, and then on toward Dawson, our destination. Crater Lake was a strange sight, perched way up on this mountaintop, and looking as fresh and blue as the Mediterranean. The vegetation here consisted of only a few stunted trees and shrub-like growths.

After a short rest we slid down the opposite side of the summit and finally reached the edge of the lake. After discussing the situation, it was decided that we women would be rowed across the lake by the Indians, while the men would hike around the edge—a measure of economy, for the Indians charged high prices for the voyage. There were three other women in the ship's company besides us two married women. The other three were of shady reputation, and had come to Alaska for an adventure. We could not of course choose our company in this land.

We waited an hour on the shore, so that we would not reach the other side of the lake before the men arrived. We wanted to walk with them from this lake to Lake Lindeman, a distance of several miles. The Indians had become angry because our men had refused to be rowed over. To show their displeasure, when we finally got into the boat, the Indians rowed fast and recklessly, and this, added to the fact that the water was getting rough, made our journey frightful. We could see a storm approaching—the storm which would have been a catastrophe had it caught us before we reached the summit. It was fortunate that we had fought against fatigue all day. As we raced over the choppy lake, we could see the men walking along, almost dead with weariness.

We reached the foot of the lake just as the men were coming over a little rise to one side. They did not stop to rest, and we hastened on as fast as we could, anxious to reach Lake Lindeman before it was too dark to find our way. We knew that this part of the country was infested with dangerous wild animals, and that it was unsafe to remain out at night. At eight o'clock we saw the dim lights of the camp at Lake Lindeman in front of us, and we hastened toward them in great relief, realizing that we had now gotten safely over the first leg of our trip to the "Inside."

CHAPTER 3

Almost a Disaster

Our joy at arriving at Lake Lindeman was almost snuffed out when on going to the only hotel we were informed by the proprietor that there was no room of any kind and that he was full to the doors. Crowds had been coming over the Pass all day and were arriving at every moment.[5] As our Indian packers had not yet arrived, we were without any means of camping, and it was now getting pitch dark and the temperature lowering.

When the proprietor noted, however, that there were women in our party, he directed us to a tent with bunks where he said we might find a place to sleep. There was no light to be seen anywhere, so we had to feel our way slowly through the blackness in order not to fall into some hole. It was beginning to freeze, with white frost forming on everything, and it was by means of the faint light coming from the frost that we finally found the tent.

---

5. More than 100,000 people are estimated to have set out for the Klondike during the gold rush. The population of Dawson City swelled to more than 30,000.

In answer to our knocks, the landlady came to the door of the tent, but would not let us in since she, too, was filled up. Luckily my husband observed a Masonic badge pinned to her dress. Relieved, he told her that he was a Mason in distress, with a wife and children who must find a place of shelter from this freezing cold. At this, she opened the door wide and bade us to come in.

Famished from the exertions of the hike, we asked about the possibilities of supper, but the woman told us that as she had been cooking all day for a lot of hungry men, she was too tired to do another thing. I told her I would get some supplies and do the cooking myself, and at this she had a change of heart. Together we began to prepare some food, while the rest of our party laid down on the ground where they were, being too tired to stand. We soon had ham, eggs, and coffee ready—a supper for the Gods! We ate voraciously.

After supper, our landlady roused several men from their bed, demanding that they give a bed to "the sick lady with the little boy." This referred to the other woman who was quite overcome by exhaustion and was ill. The men who had been deprived of their soft bed finished the night on the bare hard ground, without a blanket above or beneath them. The landlady insisted on our taking her camp bed, and herself took up a place by the stove. Thus we rested that night, my husband and I having rolled to the middle of the dilapidated bed, little Willie reposing on top of us. On the floor all about us like sacks of wheat lay tired sleepy men. What a picture for an artist—a picture replete with hardship and misery!

While we were washing the dishes the landlady told me her own story, which was typical of an Alaskan pioneer. Her husband had been a prosperous lawyer in Sacramento when the news of the gold had come, and like so many others, the stories of fabulous and easily obtained wealth had set him on fire. In former days he had been rather successful in mining, and began to think that with his experience he could go to Dawson and in six months return wealthy. With such hopes he departed with his wife to the North, leaving their only child with his parents. When they arrived at Lake Lindeman they received word that their child had died of diphtheria and had been buried immediately. They cursed their folly in leaving him behind, but they did not return to their home. Then her husband became very sick, and what with disease, sorrow and disappointment, he soon went the way of his child.

Alone now, and unable to get to the "Outside" as it was in the midst of winter, the child's mother was in misery and also became ill. However, through the friendly ministrations of those around she survived her sickness and was persuaded to open this tent hotel. Learning of her troubles, friendly Masons helped her in every way possible, and soon she was not only making a living but doing a very successful business.

I discovered that she was a wonderful woman, and she served in the capacity of mother to many lonely boys and men who through homesickness and despair needed more than anything else a little maternal tenderness. All along the way in this desolate land, we met such helpful personalities as this good woman, and were frequently cheered up by those who were willing to serve people in trouble.

During this night we hardly slept. It was storming and we could hear people arriving all during the night. The next morning on looking over the situation, we found that the outlook was not very pleasant. A bigger storm was coming up, and we had yet to make our camp. The Indians who were carrying our supplies filtered in

ERIC A. HEGG, ALASKA STATE LIBRARY (P277-001-034).

View of tent city and Lake Lindeman on June 1, 1898.

during the day, and it was not until afternoon that we set about putting up our tents so as to have a place to cook and sleep.

Lake Lindeman was crowded with people who had pretty much the same plans and work to do as we did. We were to stay here several weeks, during which we would have to build a boat to travel over the lake and down the river to Dawson. All about us were people busy constructing crude boats for the same purpose.

The next night was perhaps the first enjoyable one we had. We had unpacked and set up our little sheet iron stove, and the heat it gave off made the tent nice and warm. I cooked beans the first thing, and then made bread and apple sauce. As my husband came in from his work outside, he looked over our comfortable quarters, and then putting his arms around me, said joyously: "Joe, how happy I am tonight—how different from the despondency when I was at this same place last year, when there was no fire, cold food, damp beds, and no comforts for one who was tired, frozen and hungry."

And as we sat before the cozy warm fire eating our supper, we felt really happy. Our beds that night were infinitely more comfortable than those of the night before, even though they merely consisted of robes thrown on the rocks and gravel. Our nephew made himself comfortable in the corner of the tent. I felt rather sorry for Charlie. Everything was so coarse, crude and new to him. At first we had hesitated to bring him because of his youth, and of his always having lived in a respectable, refined and religious family where he had been sheltered from uncouthness and vulgarity.

We were just settling down to soft slumber when we were violently aroused by a terrific racket outside our very door. The confusion of noises at first made me think that there was an awful fight, but soon I began to understand what was taking place. Someone was cursing in the foulest language, and seemed to be beating his dogs. The howling, whimpering, and whinnying of the animals along with the sound of vicious blows falling made me very sick, for this was the first time I had heard men beating dogs, a phenomenon with which I later became frequently familiar in the North. The man was apparently drunk and his swearing was the worst I had ever heard, being my first acquaintance with the filthy obscenity of drunken and desperate men in the North.

At the sound of the beaten animals our Indian dog, Pete, whined and came over to us and cuddled up against our bed as if begging for protection. As I lay still, frightened and shocked, I felt my husband quietly slip out of bed, and saw him pull on his boots, pick up a stick of wood, open the tent door and disappear into the darkness. Then for a minute, I heard some loud and angry talking, and all became quiet. In a moment my husband quietly entered. I never have known what actually happened there in the night, whether my husband merely threatened or actually subdued the person. But I soon learned who the person was. Just before my husband went back to sleep, he said simply: "Well, I hope that damned author has had enough!"

This was my second impression of Jack London, and it was not a favorable one. But later I learned to forgive almost all the brutality and obscenity of intoxicated men, for what with the fatigue, cold, and hard work that was their lot, liquor was the only thing to turn to for ease and forgetfulness. The writer had just arrived and because of the darkness, the cold, and of his state of intoxication, was not successful in his efforts to set up camp, and was thus venting his dissatisfaction in the manner I have described.

Pete was uneasy and trembled during the night, and when I awoke the next morning I found Willie asleep with his arms around the animal's neck. It was very cold when we arose, with everything frozen stiff and a frosty wind blowing. Our first job was to build a roaring fire, and then repair the tent by piling rocks and dirt on the bottom flaps, which the night wind had blown up. Then, in the cold morning breeze, Willie and I went down to the lake for water to cook with, and the little fellow took great delight in thinking that he was doing something to help. I thawed out the beans of the night before, and rummaged around getting breakfast. During the process, I clumsily tipped over the stove and received quite a fright at the narrow escape of being burned out. If the tent had caught fire we would have lost everything, and in the strong wind that was blowing, a blaze could not have been stopped.

After breakfast, we took a look around and found that Jack London had moved over to the other side of the camping place, apparently pained by the reception he had received in our neck of the woods. This was the second time I had seen him move his camp as the result of an altercation. After landing in Dyea, he had had some words with a neighbor, and had moved away in his wrath. In my observations, whereas most of the men around us

Jack London in 1902 in the East End of London. Then 26, he had traveled to England to do research for his nonfictional account of conditions in the slums, The People of the Abyss.

acted very natural and affable, he seemed to assume a haughty and superior air toward the people around him.

The camp at Lake Lindeman was not very inviting. It consisted of one log hotel, several board shacks, and hundreds of tents scattered about, where campers slept and ate their meals. The place looked forlorn and God-forsaken. On one side of the lake was a vacant tree-less and shrub-less mountain waste, while on the other was a low swampy region filled with great boulders with scattered trees growing among them. An occasional bear, moose or caribou wandered into this rocky space, and these animals were little molested by the campers, whose sole attention was centered on getting to Dawson. In the camp proper, it was quite exciting watching the people making hurried preparations to leave down the lakes and river.

Everyday some party would finish its boat and would leave for Dawson. This of course made everyone else more anxious to get away. The boats that left were not large affairs, being about twice the size of a common rowboat but sufficient to accommodate a year's supply as well as two or three occupants.

At this time we bought another dog, whom we called Nig. This was our second animal, having purchased Pete, the Indian dog, at Skagway. At first there was continual war between them, Pete apparently considering himself sole proprietor of our tent when the time came to sleep. As it began to grow dark, the battle would begin, and the two dogs would fight furiously until sometimes they would even roll in the lake. Finally Nig would conquer and would go to the tent door, lie down, and show his teeth menacingly every time Pete would come near. Eventually Nig relented, allowing Pete a place inside. In a short time, however, the two dogs became the best of friends.

One day my husband rushed into our tent much excited; he had found a boat that he said he would buy for a song. The man who had owned the boat had lost his outfit on the trail, and was compelled to sell and return to the "Outside."

The craft we found was roomy enough, and served our purposes exactly. We were delighted, because this meant that we would depart at once from this dismal place. I felt sorry for the man who was compelled to sell, because he was heartbroken.

We made immediate preparations to leave. One could expect the snows any time now, and it was necessary to get to our destination before the river froze up. Even now it would rain continuously, and the water, which ran in streams down the hills, not only made everything damp and disagreeable but froze up tight at night. Now that winter was swiftly approaching, no one stopped for rain and frost, but worked hard and fast building the boats, which in many cases were crude and amateurish affairs indeed.

What began to disgust me more and more now was the brutal treatment of the dogs. The poor creatures were required to pull sleds loaded with lumber over the bare ground, a difficult task when there was no snow. The men seemed to have lost all kindness, and would whip and beat the dogs until the animals were nearly dead from fatigue and pain.

Later, I began to get used to these deplorable ways of some of the men and to realize that they were really sympathetic at heart. Life was almost more than they could stand, most of them never having been away from home before, never having had to undergo such hardships. So tired were they at night, that they would not cook anything warm to eat, and would sink down to sleep without removing their clothes. A life consisting solely of hard work, meals composed largely of beans, sourdough bread, coffee that sometimes was days old, and cold hard ground to sleep on, did not tend to develop sweet tempers.

Soon we became well acquainted with another married couple that also had a little boy. The man was an Australian named Gregory. I had been attracted to his wife, who had winsome manners and a very delicate constitution. Mr. Gregory, who knew nothing about the conditions of the North, had asked my husband to accept him as a partner while going down the river to Dawson.

After thinking the matter over, we concluded to take him and his family with us in our boat, but not to enter into any agreement of partnership. He was very thankful and gave us a good hand in getting the boat into working condition, and packing the outfits carefully in the bottom.

At this time my husband Will had 1,500 pairs of fur shoes, which he was taking to a merchant in Dawson to sell. This burden, though not heavy, was bulky, rising high over the edge of the boat. It was because of this cargo that we had first hesitated in taking aboard these people, but when Gregory begged us and made many promises, we consented to his company.

It was about noon when we were ready to set out on our voyage down Lake Lindeman to the opposite shore. There we would need to carry the boat over a short neck of land to Lake Bennett, and then be on our way down the river. A comfortable seat was made in the middle of the boat for Mrs. Gregory, while Willie and I were to take up a seat near the stern end. There was a sail in the boat, and we hoped to utilize favorable winds.

Gregory rowed, while my husband insisted on steering the craft. But I did not like the looks of the boat. It was so heavily loaded, that I felt that it was likely to tip over if anyone shifted his weight. The wind was blowing hard, and when I looked over the lake I could see that it was rough and that the waves were dashing high on the rock of the opposite shore.

My husband himself looked rather uneasy, so I began to look around for some alternative. It occurred to me that we could walk the four miles around the lake very easily by evening. On inquiring, I was told by a big Swede who was standing near that there was a good trail all the way around to the other side. That satisfied me.

Bidding them goodbye, little Willie and I started around, but had only gone a short distance when I heard Mrs. Gregory calling to me. She had concluded to walk also. We called the dogs to us, believing that they would offer some sort of protection. For quite a time the trail was very good, though it led us through underbrush, trees and sometimes swampy land.

After traveling for quite a distance, the path ended abruptly in a clearing where the men probably came for their lumber. Nevertheless, we decided to go on, for there seemed nothing else to do. The dogs were not willing to follow us through the pathless waste, so I had to continually urge and threaten them on. Sometimes they would actually lay down, and I would have to whip them mildly to make them follow. Something was wrong, and they knew it. I myself began to feel uneasy.

After several more hours of walking we were in the wilds proper, and there was no sign of any sort of trail. We thought that we had probably missed it somehow, and that if we went on as fast as we could, we would find it somewhere. I did not feel utterly lost while near the lake, so we kept in sight of the water all the time. By this time, it was necessary to carry Willie, who was getting tired. We now got ahead only by scrambling and pulling ourselves over rocks and brush. We expected all the time to get over the rocks just ahead and find the trail, but it was never there. Sometimes we would forge inland, but would be turned back by the swampy lands. Occasionally we would find trails leading from the swamps to the lake, and on examination I could discern the foot tracks of wild animals. There was no question now that the Swede had either lied or guessed.

The sun had set, and twilight was coming upon us. Turning back was out of the question, and in front of us there was no trail. I could see that Mrs. Gregory was getting very nervous and was watching me with a sort of hopelessness on her face. At times she would burst into tears.

Suddenly the dogs refused to go any further. There we were, two women and a little child, out in a desolate spot in wild Alaska and with night soon upon us. Tired in body and disturbed in mind, I sat down on a rock trying to think out what was the best thing to do. I knew that the men folks would start out to find us as soon as they reached to other side of the lake, and in so doing, would discover that there was no trail. There would soon be searching parties out for us. In the meantime it was getting darker, and we knew we would soon be at the mercy of any wild animals that might be prowling about.

As it grew darker, it became colder. If we only had a match to build a fire! That would keep us from freezing and would drive away any dangerous animals. Suddenly I remembered that I had seen Mrs. Gregory smoking that day.

"Have you a match?" I cried with both hope and fear. She immediately replied in the negative.

But in a moment she called to me in a happy voice that she had found two. This seemed to lift a great load from our shoulders, for with a fire we could not only protect ourselves but would attract the attention of anyone in search of us, or who might be passing on the lake. I had noticed a hole that had been dug nearby, which had one time been used by someone for building a boat, and I knew that this would be a good place to start a fire. Had I built a fire on the high ground, I would also have run the risk of setting the trees afire.

When I looked at those two matches in my hand, I trembled a little at the thought that in these lay our safety. I was having the disagreeable task now of quieting Mrs. Gregory, who divided her efforts between hysteria and tears. I went over to the hole, jumped in, and made a big pile of shavings and sticks, which I knew that once ablaze would make a glorious fire.

I struck the first match, and in my excitement blew it out with my own breath! I nearly fainted when I looked at that black match. Then taking the last match, with a prayer on my lips I struck it and applied the tiny flame to the shavings. They caught! As I watched the little blaze grow larger and larger, I called to Mrs. Gregory, who with a "Glory Be!" came running up. Soon we were piling larger wood on, and our fire began to leap up high and send out rays of saving warmth and light.

After our fire had been burning brightly for a time, we suddenly noticed a boat on the lake headed toward Lake Bennett. It was the regular boat making its last trip across. I told Mrs. Gregory that we must stand in front of the fire so that the crew could see that we were women alone. We tore off our coats, and waving them wildly called for help at the tops of our voices.

Our efforts were rewarded by a whistle from the boat. At first we questioned whether it was meant for us, but soon were made happy by seeing the boat turn and head for our spot.

But rescue was still far off. The shore of the lake was a mass of huge boulders over which the waves were breaking. Though the boat was now coming nearer the shore every moment, it seemed impossible that it would come near enough for us to board her.

In the dusk light it looked like a phantom ship, so much so that the dogs were almost paralyzed with fear, and howled and whined incessantly.

I realized that the captain was going through a great deal of danger in trying to rescue us. His sacrifice and the fear that he would be unable to help us through the wrecking of his ship almost put me in tears. In a short time the boat had come near enough to the rocks so that I could call to the captain. The water was so rough that I could now hear the sides of the vessel pounding against the rocks. It seemed impossible that it could come near enough for anyone to come to us or for us to get on. By the means of long poles, the crew was feeling the way through the rocks and shallow water, and thus managed to keep the boat from being dashed to pieces.

At last the boat came to a stop right next to the shore. I thought I heard the sound of someone ripping up lumber from the floor of the vessel, and a man soon appeared carrying a long piece of joist, which he had apparently torn from the flooring. With some difficulty he managed to bridge a gap between the boat and a rock on the shore. The captain called for us to come on board.

I was chosen to go over first. I experienced all sorts of fearful sensations as I walked across that shaky plank. Down beneath me I could see the water foaming and dashing against the rocks, and knew that a misstep would mean death. The next to come over were the dogs. Pete seemed thoroughly scared, and it was only after much urging that he picked his way across. Mrs. Gregory refused to come alone. She wept, and cried that she could never make it. Our calls and begging were useless.

At last the captain got angry and directed one of his men to throw a rope over to her. But still she refused to come. Finally another board was brought and the captain went over after her. He was not gentle, and tucking her under his arm said that if she uttered a word of protest he would drop her into the water. And I think he would have done so, for he was risking thousands of dollars on our behalf. The loss of his boat would have ruined him. Little Willie was the last to come across, and he seemed to think it great sport.

An hour later we landed at the wharf on the opposite side of the lake. Mr. Gregory was at the landing to meet us and welcomed us with great relief. In a moment my husband rushed up and joyously greeted us. Gregory showed his happiness by passing a bottle of whiskey around. I refused, but his wife had a good drink.

CHAPTER 4

The Ways of a Brute

When we had calmed down from our excitement and our
husbands had heard our tales, they told us that when
they had landed, thinking that we would soon join them, they had
looked around for a camping ground and had found an old deserted
cabin-hotel which would serve the purpose. They took possession,
made good fires, and laid things out for the night, hoping to have
everything ready when we arrived. When everything was settled
and comfortable, they came out to meet us.

After my husband had walked in our direction for some time he
met a woman, who when asked about the trail to Lake Lindeman
laughed at him and told him he was crazy, for there never was a
trail. Alarmed, but thinking that the woman was joshing him, he
set out to find the trail for himself. He continued in the intense
darkness that soon came upon him, and finally ran into a moose.
Scared to death now, he started back. On the way he met a man
who told him that there was actually no trail, and that there was

much danger from wild animals along the edge of the lake. By the time he reached camp he was frantic.

Seeing a boat landing at the wharf below he rushed down in hopes of persuading the captain to take him back with a party of men and search the banks for us. It occurred to him that we might have returned to the camp at Lindeman. But when he reached the wharf, he found us standing there. We were a happy bunch as we walked to our camp, my husband carrying Willie on his back, and with his arm around me. After we were settled in our cabin my husband went back to the boat to see the captain and to thank him for his sacrificial kindness in saving us from a night of suffering and possibly death. But the good fellow refused to take a cent of money for his trouble. From our meager supply, my husband selected five dollars, and thrust it into the man's pocket, and came away quickly. Despite his outward coarseness and uncouthness, this burly man who ordered his crew around like sheep showed every evidence of having the right kind of a heart. I found a great many others like him in the North.

But our happiness was marred by the disappearance of our nephew Charlie. He had gone out to search and had not returned. It was now ten o'clock, and with Charlie still out in that wilderness, I was very much perturbed as I put beans and apples on the fire for our next day's meals. I wanted to stay up, tired as I was, but my husband blew out the candle in order to make me retire. But I could not sleep, mostly because of my nephew and partly because my bed was made solely of poles placed side by side, and was thus not a comfortable affair. As I lay awake hoping and praying that Charlie would be safe, I would hear all sorts of noises outside the door and would call out his name, thinking that he was coming in.

About five o'clock in the morning I heard the door open quietly and could see the dark form of someone standing there in the room. At first, I imagined that it was a drunken man looking for a place to sleep, for the thought of Charlie had fled from my brain. My husband also heard the door open and I saw him reach under his head for his pistol, where he always kept it, but he then remembered that he had given it to our nephew. Suddenly I called out: "Charlie, is it you?"

And then, as his familiar voice answered me, I jumped out of bed, gathered the tired boy in my arms, and actually wept with thankfulness. For the first time now, he discovered that we, too, were safe.

The next morning at the breakfast table, he told us his story. After he had started out in search of us, he soon found out that there was no trail. He kept on in the darkness but found that the farther he went, the denser the underbrush became and the rougher and wilder the country. As he stumbled on, calling to us loudly every few moments, he expected at any minute to run into some wild beast. About midnight he fell down a steep bank and almost into the very coals of the fire that we had started. Nearly frozen and worn out, he guessed that we had been picked up by the regular boat to Bennett, and with fear now gone, he laid down beside the ashes and finally went to sleep. After an hour's rest, he got up and started back, suspecting that we would be worrying over his absence. He heard frequently the noises of wild animals around him, but with my husband's pistol in his hand, he was not afraid, and hastened forward as fast as possible. Thus it was that in the early morning he staggered in, his feet so sore that he could hardly stand.

Late in the morning Charlie went back to Lindeman in search of Nig, the dog who had refused to come aboard the boat. He found the animal lying on the ground where our tent had stood, apparently having smelled out his path all the way back from our fire to the previous camping ground. A man standing nearby told the boy that the dog had arrived about nine o'clock. It had required the animal eleven hours to retrace by odor our path through those boulders and brush. When Charlie brought the dog into the cabin at Lake Bennett, the animal showed a delight in seeing us that seemed strikingly human.

Though the camp we were in was called Lake Bennett, the lake proper was actually to the northeast about two miles, and the water going from Lake Lindeman to Lake Bennett rushed through a narrow gorge just to our north. Some men by means of fastening cables to their boats floated their outfits through this gorge, but the trip was hazardous, and frequently ended in the loss of some equipment. Our men decided not to risk our supplies in this way, so they set about unloading the boat and carrying our outfit and the boat overland to Lake Bennett, a task that would take several days.

While the men were thus engaged I looked the place over. Our cabin was at once a most interesting and most tragic place. Once used as a hotel, it was comprised of three rooms, but there was only one of these, about eight feet square, that fascinated me. Apparently it had once been used as a post office, for there were piles of mildewed and dirty letters laying about, which had never been opened and were without stamps. They were directed to and came from all parts of the world, as I discerned from the faintly visible addresses. I could not refrain from reading a few, for they were now never to be sent to their destinations.

This station had once been, from all the signs, the clearinghouse for mail coming in and going out. Some of the letters discarded here were addressed to individuals on the "Inside" who had met death from the many diseases and hardships that had so thinned out the masses in Dawson. Also it was here that letters sent from those in Alaska to loved ones on the "Outside" were discarded when stamps were wanting. Some were pathetic. One mother, I recall, had written her son that since he had left for the North his little sister had died, and it was necessary for him to come home at once. Another was from a wife who was scolding her husband for his folly in going into this bleak land. Probably both of these letters were addressed to dead men. Several hours in this room so distressed me that in its darkness and dampness it reminded me of a tomb filled with bygone memories and tragedies. When I came out I closed the door and nailed it tight, leaving the letters to continue to mould and decay.

The cabin had but one window, the glass of which had been broken, or stolen. The knotty logs were old, and the moss that lay on them had grown in beautiful colorful designs. It fell in festoons from the bumpy sides and from the ceiling, and made me feel as if Nature had deliberately taken this means of protecting and making beautiful what man had destroyed and made uncouth. In my mind I could see men coming in and out of this old place, some looking forward with zeal to the Far North, while others, disappointed and broken, were returning sadly to the "Outside."

After cooking the usual pot of beans and applesauce, Willie and I set out for a walk across this neck of land that stretched between the two lakes. This land was dismal, almost tree-less, and nothing but boulder-strewn, dreary hills. After sauntering along for a time,

Klondikers with a packtrain on the White Pass Trail near Bennett, British Columbia, September 6, 1898.

we climbed down a steep stretch near the lake. Here, beside a boulder and with nothing but a wooden slab as a memorial, was a lonely grave. Written on the board was the single name: "Richard."

From a man standing nearby we learned the story that led to this grave. At the time it seemed terrible but later we found it to be typical of Yukon graves. The man laying there had attempted, with his brother's help, to get their outfit through the gorge between the lakes. Their boat got away from them and was smashed on the rocks. Everything was lost. As he stood beside his brother looking at the floating wreckage, and realizing that he had witnessed the complete destruction of all his hopes and dreams, he suddenly drew his revolver and shot himself through the heart. This terrible scene nearly cost the brother his reason, but with the encouragement of the men in the camp at Bennett, who raised from their own meager stores enough money, clothing and food to supply him with an outfit, he was able to go on into Dawson. I was told that here he "made good," so that in two year's time he left this fatal country and returned to his people in Ohio.

We rummaged around some more, and farther up the hill, among some brush and old stumps, we found a few more graves. The names were gone from the slabs, and nothing but the sticks with piles of stones next to them denoted the place of these dead people who had come here with hopes but who never left. This region was considered the worst place on the trip into Dawson. Many a poor man coming through found no place to sleep here except on the bare ground. The cold winds and melting snows brought pneumonia quickly, and with morale broken by discouragements, a man was taken by death quickly.

Evil men and women seemed to have located in this place for several months before they moved on to their headquarters in Dawson for the winter. They were a tough looking set of people camping together, and had a stamp of evil on them that I soon learned to discern. They all had the same type of behavior and mannerisms, and appeared to me like vultures sitting around on trees and stumps ready at any time to pounce upon some victim and carry him away. The men were mostly gamblers and hard drinkers, while the women, mostly of the chic Frenchy type, were of the worst sort. One thing that stamped these women as bad was not so much the foul language they incessantly used but the gum they incessantly chewed. At the time, a good woman did not chew gum. But for all their ways of living, I came not so much to blame them as to pity them. Many of the women had come to Alaska with good intentions, hoping like the men to make a "stake," but finding

Men build boats beside the tent city on the shore of Lake Bennett, circa 1898.

no work, and with starvation before them, they soon slipped away from virtue. How could one blame these people for being tough? It was a tough life.

It was a cold morning when we started on our journey down Lake Bennett, expecting now to go all the rest of the way by water. As I looked back at Camp Bennett fading away in the distance, and wondering if I should ever see it again, I could not help but admit to myself that as evil and undesirable as it seemed, it was very fascinating and interesting. We dared not go fast on this lake, for it was filled with whirlpools, hidden rocks, and treacherous eddies and currents. My husband insisted on steering himself as the cargo was his, and as any indifferent hand at the rudder might bring us up on some hidden snag. Much to my relief, because of the danger at hand, he decided to take his time on the remainder of the trip. Our leisurely pace seemed to irritate Mr. Gregory, who was very anxious to get on to the gold, and who frequently said again and again, rather sarcastically, that he wanted to "get into Dawson damn quick." Under the circumstances my husband was doing the best he could, and at the impatience of his guest, he remained as usual quiet and thoughtful. Will had always been reticent in almost every situation, no matter how dramatic and serious, and I knew that he would never waste energy and words in senseless quarreling.

Toward noon, after hours of steady rowing, my husband suggested that we land for an hour and have lunch. Gregory strenuously objected to the loss of time if we beached, so we continued without any further words. Late in the afternoon the water began to get rough. We decided that it was getting unsafe to go on in the top-heavy boat, and that we would hunt for a good place to land. Rounding a corner on the north side of the lake, we saw a pretty little cove and a camping place which on one side was bounded by water and at the rear a huge cliff rose up like a shelter from the elements and wild animals.

The hot supper that night tasted especially good; then Willie and the dogs romped around and had a lot of fun after that whole day cramped up in a boat. As usual, Mr. Gregory removed himself and his wife as far from us as possible, so as not to be annoyed by the laughter and fun of the child and dogs. This night they decided to make their camp in the boat on the flour sacks, thus to avoid the discomforts of making a troublesome camp. For a man who had bragged of his many years in the Australian open, I could not account for his dissatisfaction with and distaste of camping life. For our family, camping out was a lark, and the Gregorys' flour bed rather amused Charlie and me.

This was our first night in a camp away from other people, and despite the natural protection of the towering cliff behind us, we felt a little nervous about being so far away from other people. At the camp fire, however, we were assured by Mr. Gregory, who always carried at his belt two huge revolvers, one on each hip, a sheathed knife about a foot long, and a grim row of bullets around him, that with his knowledge of weapons, we were perfectly safe from any sort of danger.

Once during the night, I imagined there was a bear in our food box, but outside of this imaginary disturbance, we slept undisturbed all night. When we opened our eyes the next morning, we were astonished to see snow all over us (we had not put the tent up the night before) and the moisture of our breaths was frozen to the fur robes next to our faces. Willie had never seen snow in such quantities before, and his excitement soon led to a little snowballing. Our playfulness annoyed Mr. Gregory, who was anxious to get started as soon as possible. He was especially disgusted when he saw the dogs pull themselves out of the foot of our beds, where they had crawled during the cold night and rolled up at our feet into snug and warm balls of fur.

After this night Willie would always beg us to let them crawl in again, and it seemed that the animals sensed his pleadings, for whenever they saw us making our beds they would come close to him and commence to shiver. And of course we always made a place for them at our feet.

Soon we were on the lake again and bound for the neck of the water called Windy Arm, a bay to the north east which led into the White Horse Rapids and then on down the river. I was enjoying the company of Mrs. Gregory very much. She aroused my sympathies because of her mouse-like timidity before her husband, and because she was never permitted to assert herself or express her opinion in the presence of her husband. I began to notice that whenever she attempted to say much, he would suddenly turn to her and give her a dominating and menacing look that would quiet her for hours. This puzzled us a little, but we concluded that such treatment of a wife by a husband was the customary thing among Australians; we attributed it to foreign ways, rather than to anything peculiar in these two people.

The day passed rather monotonously, except for another unpleasant outburst on the part of our guest. Charlie was having a busy time rowing through a treacherous current when by a sudden quirt of his oar he splashed a spray of water over Gregory. The Australian turned to him with a look of fury on his face, which ordinarily was so bland and polite, and said angrily: "Why don't you watch what you are doing?"

At this mean unpleasant remark to our young inexperienced nephew, who had so far on the trip done his best in everything, my own anger so consumed me that I could have jumped over on the Australian with all my strength. In a moment I looked at my husband, and when I saw him sitting quietly by the rudder but with a very still solemn expression on his face, I knew that he, too, was exceedingly angry. As usual, he said nothing.

About five o'clock we reached Windy Arm and found much difficulty in landing. The lake here was very rough, with a treacherous swampy shore overgrown with willows that reached over our heads. When we reached shallow water it was necessary for the men to jump out of the boat into the water hip-deep and drag us ashore. We found a good camping place here, and found

Men hauling a scow along the shore at Windy Arm in Tagish Lake, Yukon Territory, 1898.

that we had neighbors in the distance, for we could hear men talking and dogs barking occasionally. But the other campers were far enough away so that we could have a good night's rest without being disturbed by the noises of a night of loud talking, swearing and gambling. Wherever there was a camp of men to be found, one could always expect such all night sessions.

We set up our tent a little distance away from shore, not wanting to move too far away from our supplies, which if lost or stolen would mean disaster to us. When Charlie had set up the stove and was trying to get the fire started, we were suddenly alarmed to see the small cedar tree next to him suddenly burst into flames. He had built his fire too near it. Without thinking, the men grabbed our drinking water and dashed the fire out. After the excitement was over and everyone calmed down, we discovered that the men had thrown away all of our good water when they could have used the swampy water right at our feet, and of course considered it quite a joke, because it was necessary for the men to walk some distance for good water. But the circumstance and our joking afterwards greatly upset Mr. Gregory, who to show his displeasure pulled up the stakes of his tent and moved up the hill.

Soon I had some biscuits made and had cooked some rice for a change. While the savory odor of these biscuits was floating on the breeze, and our men were attacking them ravenously, I observed Mr. Gregory at his tent looking hungrily down at our feast. Knowing that Mrs. Gregory knew little about cooking, I suggested to my husband that we carry some biscuits to them. But my husband, who was rather riled at the conduct and ingratitude of Gregory by this time, replied that as they had neither chick nor child but only themselves to care for we would show them no more favors. This was agreeable to me as far as Mr. Gregory was concerned, for he had never offered a thing to any of us on the trip, but I could not help wanting to do something for his wife.

That night was the happiest one on the trip for me. I had heard so much about the dangers and as a result of the stories I had heard, had been expecting so many bad accidents that I felt exceedingly joyous that we had gotten over the worst part of our journey with so few mishaps. The air was very refreshing, and the temperatures just cool enough to make the fire feel delightful, so that all in all the evening filled me with a wonderful sense of wellbeing. The Gregorys had joined our campfire, and we were all sitting around, so that in my joy as I got up to throw some wood on the fire, I turned to Mr. Gregory and said: "Come on, let's sing a song!"

Instantly he replied by calling me a foul name. I stood there stunned. My husband immediately turned toward him and said: "*What* did you say?"

Mr. Gregory repeated his rotten phase very loudly this time. Quicker than a flash my husband was on top of him with his large hands around his throat. Gregory had not had time to pull any of his weapons in that moment, and Charlie rushed over to the men ready to jump in if Gregory attempted to reach for his knife or guns. My own sensations were peculiar, and not at all like those of the movie heroine who stands back in horror as her man is fighting. For some inexplicable reason, I wanted to jump in and help my husband if he were in danger. It was instinct rather than bravery.

But any help of mine was unnecessary for my husband was a big man and powerful. As he sat on Gregory with his fingers making the face of Gregory very purple, although he was saying nothing I knew that he was so mad that if he had had a gun (I always kept our revolver unloaded and packed away) he would have killed the man who had insulted me.

"Gregory," he finally said in a low tense voice, "if you don't stop this, I'll kill you!"

The man who was underneath began to gasp out promises and begged for my husband to stop. In a moment the two men got up, my husband with a determined look on his face, and Gregory with a sullen, whipped-dog expression. Then our guest walked off rapidly to his tent, followed by his trembling and weeping wife.

Arriving there, he immediately began to pull up the stakes, and for the second time he moved his tent up the hill. Even at this dramatic moment I could hardly keep from laughing at this cowardly way of showing his hatred.

We felt that we had had a narrow escape because we could now see that Gregory was a coward and a brute and would have shot had not my husband so quickly downed him. As my husband never carried a gun, his only defense lay in his agility. We now began to take seriously what the Australian had bragged frequently about in his stories of his life in the mines in his country. He had told us how he had driven his Negroes to work and had shot them down like dogs if they did not jump at his commands. It would be necessary to watch him carefully from now on.

We had been in our tent for only a few moments, when the timid voice of Mrs. Gregory announced her presence. She came in trembling and on the verge of tears.

"Oh, Mr. Knowles", she said tremulously, "you don't know what you've done. Mr. Gregory is a terrible man!" Her voice was low and she visibly shook. "Why, he'll kill you without warning!"

"I'm not a bit afraid of him," said my husband simply, and as if dismissing the affair began to wind his watch preparatory to going to bed. As she was leaving, I felt that I was not afraid either. We seemed to sense that once subdued, Mr. Gregory was too much of a coward to attempt anything desperate.

We were a surprised bunch the next morning when he greeted us at our tent door.

"Good morning," he said very pleasantly, just as he had always done on previous mornings. "How did you all sleep?"

Behind his gentleness now, we could see he feared that my husband would leave him behind if he did not act very decently in every way from now on. He seemed to be calculating that at the least sign of surliness on his part again, my husband would dismiss him from our company. As it was, we were lenient with him principally because of his gentle wife.

The next leg of our trip was the journey down the White Horse Rapids, and the men worked that day preparing for this hazardous journey. After lunch Mrs. Gregory and I went out for a walk, and it was on this little saunter that she disclosed the pitiful tale of her life. She told me that as she liked me and felt that she could trust me, she would unburden her unfortunate secret to me. In a secluded spot we sat down on a log, where she bent over, loosened her hair and pulled it down in front of her face so that I would not see the tears that fell continually.

"You may not believe this, Mrs. Knowles," she began, "but I have been duped into this trip to Alaska. When we left Australia, Mr. Gregory promised me and my parents that we were going to Naples in Italy to see some of his friends, and instead we came to this terrible country.

"But I will start at the beginning. I come from a very poor family in Australia, and my father had to give up his work early on account of illness. My mother therefore had to go out and do all kinds of work while I was a child so as to keep us from starvation. When I was old enough I taught school, but even with my little earnings, it was hard to supply our family with food and my father with the necessary medicine.

"One day, while I was walking rather discouraged through a park near our home, a man—this Mr. Gregory—joined me and started in a conversation. He seemed exceedingly pleasant and courteous, and very much of a gentleman, so that when he politely took his leave, hesitating a moment to ask me if I would meet him again at the same place the next Sunday, I accepted his offer of companionship.

"Soon we got to meeting every day, and I began to enjoy our walks very much, this pleasant gentleman being the first one to show me every kindness. He talked about his wealthy parents in Italy, and about the wonderful mines he owned in Australia, promising me that if I were willing, he would some day take me to see them. In my life of trouble and care all this was so fascinating to me and the splendor of it all overcame any suspicions that I might have entertained. When he asked me to marry him one evening, the thought that here was love and protection, both for me and my parents, made me accept him in perfect faith.

"Before he left me, he handed me five hundred dollars to give my parents. I had been rather ashamed of my secret meetings with this man, and had as yet not told my parents about him. His plan was for us to take ship the next day to Italy to get the blessings of his folks.

"When I got home that night I wrote my mother a long letter, telling her everything and asking her forgiveness. All night I could not sleep and at times went up to her room planning to rouse her and tell her everything. But as I looked at her and my father sleeping there, I lost courage and merely knelt by their bed and prayed for them. This was our first parting, and though Mr. Gregory promised that we would return a few weeks after our marriage, I felt very badly about leaving them. In the early morning I packed a few things and stole quietly out of the house.

"At the wharf Mr. Gregory met me, and taking me aboard ship showed me my stateroom filled with flowers and books. I imagined myself the happiest girl alive, and looked upon my future husband as being pure and good. How soon was this all to change!

"After we had been out to sea two days, he came to my stateroom without that angelical look upon his face. He told me everything then. In very plain terms he explained that he had never intended to go to Naples, but that we were on our way to Alaska. On the ship's register our names were signed, 'Mr. Gregory and Wife.' When he said that if I ever told a soul, he would *kill me*, I was so humiliated and horror-stricken that I fainted away. When I came to I was lying in my berth.

"Oh, Mrs. Knowles, I have suffered a thousand deaths since I have left home. Mr. Gregory is a brute, and many times I have been afraid that he would kill me. He has told me frequently that if I ever told anyone of my troubles he would feed my body to the dogs. I know that he will never marry me, and that I can only look forward to a life of shame."

Suddenly we heard the sound of voices in the distance. "Mrs." Gregory said, "Quick! Let us go back. The men are calling. Some time, if I have a chance I will tell you more."

When we reached camp, we found that we were to go by boat again and try to put some more miles behind us before night. That night we landed at a little mining camp where we found everyone greatly excited. There had been a new strike not forty miles away, and many of the men who were on their way to Dawson were going to the diggings to try their luck.

Suddenly it occurred to me that here was the place to get rid of this Gregory, and when I mentioned my idea to my husband, he replied that he had been thinking the same thing. We had decided that after the fight of the night before, our further association would be dangerous. When I related the sorrowful tale of Gregory's companion to my husband that night, in his quiet way he said that he could get rid of this brute the next day without arousing any suspicions. But poor Mrs. Gregory!

After breakfast the next morning, my husband and Charlie went down to the boat where Mr. Gregory had made his camp. Accosting the Australian in an earnest way, my husband asked

Gregory if he would like to buy the boat, for we had decided to go to the new diggings. Gregory refused immediately, saying that he had already decided to go to the new mining district himself.

When I heard this, I almost shouted with joy, and Charlie was so delighted at the way Gregory had fallen for our ruse that he had to turn and walk away in order to keep the Australian from seeing the happiness and amusement on his face. It would not have been safe if Gregory had suspected that we were merely trying to get rid of him.

In a short time the men were working at getting Mr. Gregory's things out of the boat and onto the bank. It was necessary for them to wade in the water and carry the goods by hand from the boat. At any moment, my husband later told me, he was afraid that Gregory would back out of the bargain and want to go with us.

In a little while our family was aboard and the Gregorys were ashore, and we were very anxious to be off before the Australian would change his mind. Just as we were pulling away, we heard him shout to us, calling for us to wait, and he came running out in the water to us as fast as he could. Those were bad moments for us as we saw him approaching. But when he got to the boat's edge, he put his hand out very pleasantly and shook hands with each of us, bidding us all a cordial good-bye.

Relieved as I was, I do not think that my farewell was said very pleasantly. We were all like happy kids as we pulled away from that camp. It was a "dirty trick," I know, to have to get rid of that brute the way we did, but it was advisable, I think, for peace.

CHAPTER 5

Rapids on the Way to Louse Town

The White Horse Rapids were before us. As we came near this gorge—through which the waters from the lakes flowed with tremendous speed and noise, dashing against high boulders, whisking over shallow shoals, and piling up against the banks— my husband, who was harboring memories of twice going through this place, became more and more uneasy. When I gestured that I wanted to go through these rapids with him, he gave an emphatic no, which settled the question definitively.

Before this gorge there were many people with barges and boats waiting, and they were an impatient and angry crowd. Going through this channel required the dexterity and knowledge of the natives, whose services were now so much in demand because of the great rush of travelers and merchandise going through before the river would close for the winter that it would be necessary for one to wait perhaps for days before he could get a pilot.

Like all the rest of the anxious crowd that was waiting here, we expected to be held up for some time. Then, looking over the people

Three men navigate the White Horse Rapids.

in the crowd, my husband suddenly discerned Jimmy, the Indian pilot who had taken him through the rapids two years[6] before, and to whom he had taken a liking. In a short time the Indian had come to us, greeted my husband cordially, and promised to take him through the rapids immediately.

Willie and I had the four-mile walk around the rapids now before us. But just at the beginning of the channel I watched my husband, my nephew Charlie, and the Indian begin to shoot down on the rushing water. We saw them go through the worst part in safety and then, feeling rather weak from excitement and fright, began our journey. All the time we could hear the tremendous

---

6. It was actually the previous year.

roar of the waters, and could picture our men rushing down this gorge, which with perpendicular walls on each side and great rocks laying about, looked as if a gigantic plow had torn its way through the very mountain. Though of course we managed to get lost again, we finally reached the other side after an exhausting scramble through brush and fallen trees. The roar of the water had so frightened the dogs that they cringed by our side with their tails between their legs.

After the men had made camp, my husband started out to meet us, and we were thankful to find each other safe. That evening while we were waiting for the biscuits to cook, our attention was drawn to a tiny moving speck way up on the mountainside. At first we thought that it was deer, but as it came nearer we saw that it was really a man coming down to us, and we finally discovered that he was an Indian. My husband, seeming to understand the reason for his visit, went to meet him.

As soon as they came together into the camp, I saw that the Indian was carrying a very dirty object in his hand, which at first I thought was the head of some animal. He cut off a piece and handed it to me. I discovered now that it was a piece of meat, but so encrusted with dirt that I immediately told my husband I could never clean it. Nevertheless my husband handed three cigars to the Indian, who was so delighted by the bargain that he walked happily away. He had walked all day with this chunk of meat, throwing it down on the ground whenever he rested. He had hoped to find some white man who would give him whiskey or tobacco for it. The Indians in the North never take money for their game, but want, rather, liquor or tobacco or bright colored jewelry, or perhaps some fascinating piece of clothing, like a white collar two or three sizes too big. With his pocketknife my husband carved off the dirty portions of the meat, which he gave to the dogs, and we put the rest on to fry. How that meat melted in our mouths, after being so long without fresh meat! How infinitely delicious and how we regretted not cleaning and eating the parts we had thrown to the dogs!

The next day we sailed down the river feeling very happy over our good fortune so far and over our associations, which since the departure of the Gregorys were happy indeed. The river here was wide but in its center was a very swift current which raced forward at six miles an hour. Rowing and with our sail up, we went a great deal faster than before. A happy crowd we were as we sped down this lane of current singing "Sailing Down the River in Our Little Birch Canoe."

The mountains around us looked as if they had been painted by the lavish brush of some human hand, for here and there were brilliant red soils, and occasionally on the naked slopes there were streaks of bright blue and green as if one had carelessly thrown buckets of paint against the rocks. The banks were carpeted with great mats of moss, which in places were a foot deep, and the only other signs of vegetation were scattered brush and occasional pine and birch trees that bunched up here and there.

But our peace was short, for soon we approached the Five Fingered Rapids, a stretch through which the water rushed furiously, but where with good judgment and good seamanship one might pass through the island-spotted channel with safety. My husband had gone through this place twice before, and decided to attempt it by himself this time. He called to us to lay low in the boat and hang on tightly to something while we were swept down this rough lane. We were five minutes going through, and the occasional glimpses

Roping a steamer through Five Finger Rapids, circa 1899. Men with rope help a riverboat negotiate the narrow channel while other people watch from high on the rocks.

I got of my surroundings were sufficient to show me that we were whizzing between two high bluffs and that if we struck either one at the speed we were going, we would come to our end. Each time a wave crashed aboard Willie would give a wail that also expressed my own feelings. When we had gone through the most dangerous part, a glance at my husband told me that he himself was "scared stiff." His face was white, and I could actually see his knees shaking, while the hand that held the steering rod was trembling unsteadily. From now on, our trip to Dawson was comparatively uneventful as far as dangerous rapids were concerned, but we nevertheless had to keep our eyes open for other dangerous places in the river.

One evening we were attracted to a very beautiful place for our camp. In a sudden curve of the river lay a small island that fitted our purposes exactly. The trees here were tall, slender and majestic, and on everything lay the colorful brown and golden leaves of fall. The trunks of the trees were of a silvery gray hue that made our surroundings look rich.

We laughed at Charlie's plan to go fishing for our meal, because one seldom catches fish in the Upper Yukon. He had only been gone ten minutes, when with a cry he ran into camp holding a very large salmon in his hand. He told us that he had hardly set his line when it had given him such a jerk that he almost went into the river. This fish offered us considerable entertainment that evening. While Charlie was talking, he suddenly looked down and found a minnow only three inches long on his line. With his mouth and eyes open in amazement, he held the little fish before his face. The miracle was soon explained when we found the large fish flopping away from us on the ground. It had been a case of the minnow swallowing the hook and the big fish swallowing the minnow. Apparently the large fish had sensed that he had been captured unfairly, for when he lay sizzling in the frying pan, he suddenly disappeared. After a moment's search, we found him hiding under the stove. But for all his attempts to escape, he soon disappeared down our throats, and he was a delicious morsel indeed in this land of canned goods.

About twelve o'clock that night my husband and I were startled out of our bed by the frightened cry of Charlie.

"Uncle Will!" he gasped in the darkness, "Look, look, the trees are on fire!"

My husband answered with a hearty laugh.

"Those are the northern lights, Charlie," he called to our nephew.

I looked with amazement. The sky above us was all bright with rolling and tumbling clouds of vapor through which every color of the rainbow was playing. At first it looked as if the tinted masses of vapor were piling upward toward the zenith, and then they would rush away in long ribbons of color. Suddenly it all disappeared. This was my first experience with the Aurora, but I was to become familiar with and almost indifferent to this phenomenon before I left the Yukon.

The next morning the first birds I had seen since I had come in from the "Outside" flitted down into our camp and almost carried the biscuits out of the pans in which they had been cooked. Of a light blue color and about the size of pigeons, these birds were so tame that we could almost touch them, and they seemed not in the least afraid, watching every one of our movements with intelligent curiosity. In this land where there seemed to be no bugs or worms, I imagined that the poor birds were very hungry, but my intention to throw them bits of bread dough was cut off by my husband's reminder that flour cost ten dollars a small sack.

The position of the sun began to interest me, and to give me strange sensations after having always seen it come up in the east and go down in the west. Up here, however, it would only come up in the south and then rest all day on some mountain crest. Then it would fall off at night and disappear. The sky began to take on a twilight hue and appeared to get smaller the farther north we went. What little sunshine there was reflected from the water with such intensity that we all became painfully sunburned, and soon took on a tan that made us look like Indians.

We had now been traveling down Lake Lebarge for several days, and as we approached the foot of it and prepared to enter the

Two men in boat going through the rapids on One Mile River between Lake Lindeman and Lake Bennett, circa 1898.

river proper, the current became very swift and dangerous again. Landing to camp now became a hazardous task. When we wished to land, everyone would sit tense, and then at a signal from my husband, Charlie would pull for shore with all his strength.

It was after one such exciting landing one evening that I sank down exhausted under some tall pine and birch trees that gave our camp a placid and almost heavenly aspect, and I was suddenly struck with the vacantness, the void of this forsaken country. As I looked up though the green needles mixed with golden leaves at the blotches of sullen sky above me, I recalled the agonizing story told to me some time before by a woman. It was a story of past wealth, spoiled children, the suicide of a son, the ingratitude of daughters, the failure of her husband and his death, and then her own advancing age spent in sorrow and destitution. When she had finished her tale, she cried to me, "Oh, if I could only go to some place where there was not a living soul, not an animal, where I could not hear even the song of a bird or the sound of any living creature!"

As I lay there on the thick moss, it occurred to me here was the place for that poor tired soul. I dug into the moss with my hands and could not find a bug of any description. Since I had left the "Outside," except for the two "robber" birds, I had not seen a living creature of any kind, not even a fly. Except for the distant sound of the men chopping wood, and the swish of the river, there was no sound of any description. For all those who crave the most abject solitude, there can be no more ideal place.

We had not yet finished with near-catastrophes on our trip to Dawson. After we had supperd one evening, then put on the pot of beans and a kettle of dried apples, and had made a pan of bread, we went confidently to sleep. As there was danger of someone landing and stealing our boat, we had taken the precaution not only of firmly fastening the boat to a stump but of tying Pete the dog inside the boat, knowing that he would make a fuss if anyone approached. It had been our habit when any of us awoke during the night to replenish the fire, look things over and go back to bed. But this night, none of us awoke.

"Oh, uncle, look quick! Hurry!" was the cry from Charlie that jerked us out of bed in the freezing dawn. We saw our nephew running down to the shore. There was our boat slowly floating out into midstream! In a few moments it would reach the rapid current in the middle and would be whisked downstream to be smashed on the rocks below.

In a moment I saw the men running, wading, splashing out into the water with every ounce of energy they possessed. The boat had just reached the current and had started to move away when my husband grasped the rope and held. The frightened dog was running frantically about, barking, and showing his teeth in delight over the rescue.

When the men got the boat back the mystery was solved, for the rope that had fastened the boat to shore had been chewed in half by the dog! Had our boat gotten away we might have never been rescued from this isolated spot, and it was many miles over trackless wastes to any town. We might never have survived this misfortune, for there was little food or sympathy for destitute people in the North.

Our arrival at Fort Selkirk marked the last lap of the trip to Dawson. At this place the Canadian Mounted Police were stationed for the serious task of examining every individual going to Dawson and seeing if he had his necessary money and food supply for the winter. As there were no extra supplies in Dawson, anyone without the allotted amount was prevented from going further than Selkirk.

This place was also a great trading station where the Indians sold their furs to people going "Inside." My husband wanted to get enough fur for a coat, but though he had money, the Indians would not accept it. What they wanted was tobacco, jewelry or whiskey. My husband had his eye on five marten skins, but could find no trinkets or tobacco or liquor with which to obtain them. An old brass chain fastened to his watch caught the attention of an Indian, who accepted this relic for the fur and appeared delighted with the bargain.

As I was always inquisitive regarding graves and burying places, when I heard of the Indian burying ground at Selkirk, I gathered up Willie and went to see it. The cemetery was situated on a high knoll, and to get there we had to crawl up over a steep stony slope. I cannot imagine how the Indians got their dead up this rocky flight. At the top we were struck with an unusual sight. The dead were hanging in the air, that is to say, they were suspended in little houses that looked like dog kennels raised up on poles. Feeling guilty and a little afraid, we climbed up a steep ladder and peered into one of the houses. There on the floor inside lay a jumble of rags, bones, toys, trinkets, and a skull. Someone before us had taken a stick and had pushed these gruesome things around.

As we were looking fearfully into this death house, we suddenly were paralyzed by the sound of a voice calling to us! Willie and I scrambled down the dilapidated ladder, and hit every high spot all the way down the hill. We were sure that the Indians were after us, and did not plan to linger around and get scalped. Just as I passed under a tree, I felt something grab me by the hair and at that moment I slipped, expecting death at any moment. When I dared to get up and look around, I found my hair caught on a branch, and looking up the hill, saw my husband standing on a rise and laughing as if he were having a spasm. As a result of this experience, I seemed to lose interest thereafter in graves of any sort, Indian or otherwise.

Just before leaving Selkirk, I witnessed a fight between two men. Except for the scene at the wharf at Dyea, I had not seen any real fistfights, but I later became used to seeing men "go to it." The main cause of fights, such as the one at Selkirk, was over dogs. In this case, an "Outside" dog of a "musher" (a professional driver of dog teams) started a fight with a set of malamutes belonging to another musher, in the midst of which, the owner of the single dog, a large, strong, rough-looking man, waded into a combat and began to kick the malamutes. The other musher, a slender man, remonstrated and in a moment the men and dogs were all mixed up in a terrific battle. A crowd of people immediately gathered, standing by silently watching the fight with interest. The fighting men looked very ugly, and I was afraid that one would pull a gun and shoot the other. But my fears were allayed when the big man ended it suddenly by hitting the smaller man so violently, that the little fellow was laid out flat, and was carried into a saloon nearby in an unconscious state. Soon the bystanders separated the dogs, and peace reigned. The fight was very disgusting and horrible to me, but interesting.

Now we were on the Yukon River and were looking forward eagerly to our arrival in Dawson. As we had left Lake Lebarge with its daily gales, peculiar currents, and rough waters, we were feeling gay as we rowed and sailed down the river.

In our cargo we had a small table, which I blush to confess I had borrowed from the deserted hotel at Lake Bennett, where it would have rotted away. As we were serenely departing from Selkirk, we turned suddenly into the current, and off went the table from the top of our supplies. Despite our efforts we could not reach it in the swift current, and as I watched it for an hour or so floating around with its four legs sticking up in the air, I felt badly because I had heard there was no furniture or lumber in Dawson.

All the way going down the river we met or passed people going to Dawson. There was one fellow in particular who irritated us with his loud bragging. He was rowing a barge filled with merchandise, and was so tickled over his superior seamanship that whenever he passed us he would draw our attention to it in an uncouth way.

"Never mind," my husband frequently remarked, "he's not in Dawson yet."

One morning as this man passed us, my husband asked him if he had an extra piece of rope, which we needed badly. The man replied insolently that he would neither give, lend, nor sell. Late in the afternoon, as we were turning a bend in the river, here was this man, stuck fast in a sand bar. He was frantic with distress and seeing us, called loudly to come to his rescue. It was sort of an unwritten law up here to help people out of such distress, and we had already helped others out of similar difficulties, despite the danger one incurred by trying to stop near a dangerous sand bar. There were many such shoals in the river, but by careful scrutiny of the surface of the water and the direction of the currents, one could avoid them.

"This is a fine time to teach this man a lesson before he gets into Dawson and is taught some other way," my husband remarked. So we sailed by him, quite indifferent to his yelps of distress. We did not like to do this, but thought that because of his overbearing ways, this man's life could be in danger among miners who are made bitter and without patience from the cold, fatigue and disappointments, and that he could not fail to understand now that his own bragging and carelessness had brought him to this misfortune.

Our journey was now beautiful, and as we were fast approaching our destination, we drank in every beauty with extra gusto. In the morning, when the sun rose and sat upon some mountain to the south, in the clear atmosphere it looked like a great ball of flame. All about us were beauteous colors, from the soils that showed in

A view of a steamboat traveling up the Yukon River toward Dawson.

the rough hills, from the moss and leaves that took on every hue, and from the water itself, which in the later afternoon looked like a flowing stream of burnished gold.

Once while we were singing "Way Down Upon the Suwannee River," we suddenly heard the same voices, the same tune, the same words sing to us from the hills. We counted three distinct echoes, and then the sounds seemed to vanish over the mountaintops. We sang all day and were awed at times by the marvels of this whispering atmosphere.

Sometimes in the afternoon when there was no wind blowing, it would get hot and sultry. It was late one such afternoon that we hung to the right bank to keep off the low rays of the sun, and at the sight of a cool island on the other side, I suggested to my husband that we go there to camp. But my husband had been looking at the cliff there, and said that he saw a huge fissure at the top, and that he did not like the looks of it, so that we had better go on. I pooh-poohed his suspicions, and gave up only reluctantly, while he directed Charlie to row to the other side of the river opposite the cliff.

A half hour later when we had lost sight of that place, having gone around a bend in the river, we heard a terrific noise—as if the very bottom of the river was shaking. Waves large enough to make our boat rock came down the river, and for some time the waves formed in small whitecaps that danced in the sunlight. We surmised that there had been a landslide somewhere.

That evening a party of men who passed by our camping place stopped long enough to tell us that the whole cliff we had seen had fallen into the river, and that the river changed its course and was now flowing over the very island on which I had wanted to camp. This would naturally have been the end of us.

We were now but four days from Dawson, and would soon reach Forty Mile, a little mining settlement where we planned to remain for several days. We arrived at this place quite late at night, and were anxious to get into a cabin immediately for the weather had changed very fast in the last few days, and by the excessive cold that began to pervade everything we knew that winter was arriving fast. The town consisted of several log cabins, some campers' tents, and one log hotel. The hostelry was rather dilapidated, having one door and a glass window that had been broken by some bullet. Now the elements were kept out by a piece of muslin stretched across the opening. The proprietor, as we expected, told us that every room, bed, and all the floor space was occupied, but when he saw a woman and a child in the party, he seemed very anxious to help find a place for us to sleep.

"I know of a log cabin," he said, "which has not been occupied for some time, and if you'd like to use it I'll take you to it."

We asked him why it was unoccupied when there were so many men sleeping around us outdoors without a tent or shelter of any kind. As we stumbled through the darkness, he told us.

The fall before, two very young and inexperienced people—a delicate man and a beautiful and refined woman—had come alone down the river and had stopped at Forty Mile. Educated and probably from good families, they did not mingle with the people in the settlement but stayed in their cabin, and were only seen when they gathered wild cranberries together, and when cutting wood for the fire. One night about twelve o'clock when everyone was asleep, the sound of a pistol shot roused everybody, and then the sound of a second shot was heard. Everyone rushed out to see what was the trouble, but not a soul was in sight. A light was shining in the cabin where the young couple lived. After people knocked at the door and got no response, the door was pushed in and disclosed the young man and woman lying dead on the floor. A revolver was clasped tightly in the man's hand.

There was nothing in the room by which to identify them, and the reason for this apparent suicide pact was only divulged when the contents of the room were examined. They were found penniless and without a thing to eat. They probably had not eaten any food except berries for days. It was concluded that they had traded their boat to an Indian for the cabin, where they could get out of the cold. When they had run out of supplies, they were probably too proud to ask for food, and as the young man could find no work or means of finding assistance, the two decided that the easiest way out was death.

"Yonder is the cabin," finished the hotelkeeper, pointing in the dark. "No one seems to want it after the two people killed themselves in it."

As we were not superstitious to the point of remaining out in the cold when this shelter could be obtained, my husband offered to pay for the days we would occupy it. Remarking that the cabin did not belong to him, and for us to take it as long as we wanted it, the hotelkeeper handed us a candle to find our way through the underbrush, and then disappeared. Our candle went out, but after staggering around in the darkness, we finally found the lonely and silent cabin. I was left alone in that fatal room while Will and Charlie went down to the boat and carried up our outfit.

After a warm fire was built, the beds made, and the beans and apples put on to cook, we found this abode very comfortable, despite its history. It is curious how hot coffee and a good supper dispel one's superstitions and fears. A little courage was necessary, however, in going to sleep after hearing that terrible story, but once asleep, we were so tired that not one of us woke until morning.

After we had neatened things up the next morning, Willie and I left this dismal place, and after following the men around for a while went to pick cranberries. We found the berries so sweet and sugary that I put up several quarts of jam. We gathered all of this fruit we could, for it was a luxury in this place, and I felt that I should put up all I could gather.

Forty Mile was a bleak and dreary place. The mountains are far from the river here, and except for low scraggy trees and underbrush, the place looks deserted and unkempt. The Indians had trapped and killed game for miles around, but farther back in the mountains, where no white men ventured because of the chances of getting lost and freezing to death, wild animals could still be found. The snow had fallen for several days on the mountains, and on the day after our arrival it snowed all the time, making the ground soft and slushy. During the long nights the howl of the malamutes made one feel as if he were far away from all human habitation.

We left this place early one morning when everything was so dark that we could hardly find the boat, and when there was not a star or light to be seen. We were now wearing our heavy clothes and fur robes, and the men could only keep warm by rowing the boat. There was one day before us to Dawson—Dawson!—our goal and our hope, the headquarters of evil, of fortune, and, for many, of despair! Anxious as we were to get into Dawson that night, we failed to reach it, and as evening approached we found that we were still several miles away. Very late in the evening we found that it was necessary to land at the outpost of Dawson, a little town with a forbidding name—Louse Town. Tomorrow we would be in Dawson!

CHAPTER 6

Dawson

It was pitch dark when we beached at Louse Town. The air was intensely cold, so we hastened to erect a crude camp next to the water's edge, being too fatigued to carry our equipment up over the high bank. The faint twinkle of lights in the blackness told us that we were now near civilization, and that the days on the river were over. Despite the dangers and anxieties on the river, we were now somewhat loath to leave it, for it had carried us safely to our destination.

The howling and fighting of dogs roused us in the early morning. We rushed out of our tent and rescued Nig and Pete from several Indian dogs from the town, and returning, slept the sleep of the dead for several hours more. Eventually we dragged ourselves out and went to look over our new homeland.

In the distance and across the river from Louse Town lay Dawson, which was a crude gathering of log houses and tents. It could hardly be called an imposing place, being rather a cluster of rough hovels arranged irregularly in what might be called streets.

Everything was dark and gloomy because the sun was now gone, and the cold grey sky seemed as if to lie sullenly on the surrounding mountains. Snow lay on the ground. With a quiet swish the waters of the river murmured by.

My hands were full in keeping Willie in the tent long enough to dress him. He realized that at last he could run and romp with the dogs on land as long as he pleased, and he was anxious to start in. All the anxiety that was in our minds at the beginning of each new day while on the river was now absent at this first breakfast in Dawson, and we ate our humble meal chatting happily in anticipation of what our first day in Dawson would bring to us.

My husband now told me that he would have to look around for a place to live. He and Charlie started out for Dawson soon after breakfast and left me to look after our belongings. As I sat there alone in the tent, the realization of all that we had gone through in our last two months came to my mind, and I spent a few minutes in a prayer of thanks to Him who had brought us safely through to Dawson. I was very anxious to get settled and to get everything ready and as comfortable as possible for the swiftly approaching winter. Already it was almost impossible to keep warm in the tent.

About noon my husband returned with the discouraging news that he could not find a cabin of any kind in either Dawson or Louse Town that we could use for the winter. He had discovered, however, a place we could move into temporarily. It was a cabin belonging to a man my husband had known previously who was now gone up to the mines. No one knew when he would return, so we decided to move in until he returned.

We made our way into the crude town of dilapidated tents and cabins and soon came to the door of the cabin that we were to call home. Luckily the door was not locked, so I pushed it open and stepped in. What a dismal and dirty place it was! The interior was very dark, for there was only one window and it was so dirty that little light entered through it. The floor, I could see, consisted of eight inch boards simply laid on the ground. In places there were cracks between the boards large enough for one to put a finger through. I could see plainly that all of the sweeping was done into the cracks and not out the door. The floor, however, showed little signs of having been swept for it was very black and dirty and looked as if it had not been cleaned for years. The walls were made of logs and the cracks between them were filled with moss. The moss had grown and now hung in long streamers over the logs. As the logs had aged, the grain of the wood had come to stand out in the most beautiful colors. When we lit our candles, the beautiful blotches of brown and gold on the logs glistened through the moss, which now gracefully swayed like dancing fairies before the gentle breeze that came in through the open door.

This cabin in which we now made our home was the oldest cabin in Dawson and had been built by Indians a half a century before. We were not situated in the main part of Dawson but in the suburb which had been humorously named Louse Town. My husband decided to remain here until we could find a cabin over in Dawson proper. The task of cleaning out this place seemed too great for the short time we would probably stay, so we made things look real home-like merely by stacking the canned goods on the shelves, by building a fire, and by stacking our boxes around the room. By setting up a board before the window, I managed to construct a crude dressing table. Our beds were luxurious as compared to the rock-strewn and frozen ground that had been our bed for so long.

ERIC A. HEGG, UNIVERSITY OF WASHINGTON LIBRARIES, SPECIAL COLLECTIONS (HEGG 2280).

A view of Klondike City, which the miners often called Louse Town, in winter, circa 1898.

The beds were made of poles placed side by side to form a flat place on which I laid our bedclothes for the coming night. The table there was so unstable that we ate lunch with it resting upon our knees.

During the afternoon of this first day, the men were gone and I unpacked everything. The floor discouraged me because of its filthy condition. There was probably not a brush or broom in Dawson. Cleaning clothes was out of the question. True, I had two dishcloths, but these had to last a year, and when they were worn out, there would be no others. Finally with everything arranged I sat down on a box and looked over the result. We now had a really home-like place in this cold discouraging land! Beans and applesauce bubbled and steamed on the stove. The dogs lay sleeping comfortably on the floor with Willie, who, also asleep, reposed peacefully with his head resting on the rising and falling side of one of the animals. As I sat there quietly, I wished I could paint a picture of this sleeping group and show in rich color Willie's yellow hair that curled all over his head and fell down his shoulders in soft curls. When the men stepped in at the door, they were taken aback by the homeyness of the scene.

"Why have you gone to all this trouble, Joe, when you may have to pack everything up again?" Will asked me.

The thought of leaving this cabin, which I had now become greatly in love with, made me weep. Here, Willie and I would be very comfortable, having the river right near us to keep us company while the men would be away. My husband, guessing how badly I was feeling, suddenly picked me up and sat down on a box with me on his lap. Before he could speak, the box gave way and the two of us landed on the dogs and Willie. Nig the Indian dog jumped up and bit Pete, the other dog, who ran whining under the bed. Charlie had jumped at our crash and nearly tipped over the stove. Little Willie, with wide-open eyes, said that he had dreamed that the boat had turned over.

And then, after all the confusion was over, my husband said to me rather gleefully, "All I wanted to tell you, Joe, was that I have just seen Mr. Martin, my friend who owns this cabin. He told me that we could have the cabin for as long as we wanted and that he would come down immediately and move his stuff away."

This was wonderful news, for it meant that we were to have a warm and comfortable shelter during the freezing winter. Few people were as fortunate as we, and many had to live outdoors in tents with little fuel to keep them warm.

A view of Front Street in Dawson City in 1898. The businesses along the street included the Pioneer Bakery and Café, Hegg Photos and Views, the Northwest Trading and Commission Co., and the Globe Saloon.

Willie and I went down to the river the next day and gathered willows. These when tied together made a most effective broom, and I was able to do wonders with it when cleaning out the dirt in our home. On our way back from the water, we looked over the country. Louse Town itself was nothing more than a collection of huts and tents on one side of the river and was looked upon as a sort of suburb of Dawson, which was about a half-mile distant across the stream. Though it was the mining metropolis of the north, Dawson was no sumptuous town. One long main street bordered the Yukon River and the other thoroughfares of the town were merely trails and paths that wound their way through the crude shacks, tents, and houses. Some of the houses were made of logs, like ours, but building from this scarce material had long since stopped, and most of the miners lived in tent houses. Timber and wood to burn had been long ago cleaned out of the immediate environs of Dawson and one had to go a long distance to obtain it. Hence what was brought in was used for fire and not for building purposes. As a result, the houses were crude and cold structures. Made mostly of canvas, they were very small, so small, I discovered, that some of the residents had to take down the stove at night in order to find a place to put the bed.

About the first of October, the Yukon River closed for the winter. It was a most amazing and spectacular sight. For days I stood on the riverbank and watched the river, which was beginning to fill with ice. At first the ice cakes floated smoothly down the current, bobbing gracefully up and down on the moving surface. But as the days passed and became colder, great chunks of ice would pile up near the banks; then they would suddenly loosen and the river would move smoothly and swiftly again. Later still, the cakes piled up more and more so that the river at times would be a solid mass of tumbled ice. Occasionally the glistening mass would bulge up in the center and I would see before me a large mountain of ice. At these times the Klondike River, which lay between Louse Town and Dawson, would rise dangerously. This damming up of the Klondike and sometimes of the great Yukon itself was greatly feared by the Dawson people. Several times during previous years the swirling ice and water had rushed over the banks of the Yukon, descending upon and sweeping away part of the town proper. Even as I watched it, I was sometimes terrified by the spectacular jamming up of the ice and then the sudden giving way of the jam, accompanied by a deafening booming and cracking of the great cakes.

One afternoon, as my husband stood by my side silently watching the tumbling and piling of the ice, he said: "The Yukon will probably close before tomorrow morning!"

During that afternoon I was startled to hear calls for help coming from out on the river. Looking over the swiftly moving field of frozen hunks that intermittently heaped up in places, I saw some men in a boat about 200 feet away who were struggling with all their energy to make a landing. Even I could realize that they were in great danger and that they would have to be aided if they were to be saved from being crushed among those heavy and razor-edged blocks of ice. I ran up and down the bank pleading with various people to go to the rescue of these men, but I soon saw that to reach them would have been impossible. Any boat that would venture out into the stream would have been as bad off as the one already out there, and no one cared to flirt with death to the degree of jumping from one cake of ice to another in an effort to reach these unfortunates. At this point of the river the water ran six miles an hour, with the result that it could not freeze smoothly but would only become solid and stable after a severe jam. Help, therefore, at this point was considered impossible.

Sick with the thought of the fate of these men, I had hardly energy to get supper. I had heard them crying for help for a long time after they went by our cabin, and the distress of their voices kept ringing in my ears. My husband pointed out that they had a chance to get to land below Dawson where there was a bend in the river. I do not remember whether I discovered what eventually happened to these men, but my impression now is that they were saved.

We were jerked out of our slumber during the night by another yell of "Help! Help!" and our men dressed hastily and ran out into the darkness down to the river. The river was now in an even more dangerous mood, and the menfolk had to stand by uselessly, listening to the heart-breaking shrieks for help. The boatmen were probably crushed to bits during the night. I found out later that such disasters were fairly common during the closing of the river, and that wreckage of the victims—men who had made the fatal error of starting too late in the season for the land of gold— was frequently found on the banks of the bend in the river below Dawson. Bits of boats, clothing, and bodies told of a terrible death.

The next afternoon Willie and I witnessed the closing of the river for the winter. Suddenly we heard a thunderous grind and crunching of the large cakes of ice and saw them pushed and piled on top of each other until the river was a tumultuous mass of tumbled ice. Everything was now quiet as death until suddenly the mass began to bulge up weirdly in the middle and the river looked like a chain of white icy hills. And then that desolate stillness settled on everything again. The sound of the rippling and swirling water was gone for many months.

The sun had set for eight months and with only the reflected light from the sky to throw a mild twilight upon this whole chaotic picture, it seemed as if an evil loneliness had come upon everything. As I took Willie by the hand and went into the cabin, I began to feel depressed and sad. Here we were buried in a remote land for eight months to come. If anything dreadful should happen to my little girls in California, I could not get to them—perhaps I would not hear of it. As I began to lapse into a downcast state of nervousness as a result of these disturbing thoughts, I soon saw the silliness and futility of this way of thinking. It was then that I determined not to let the thought of death or any other disastrous thing enter my mind about the little ones on the "Outside."

Nevertheless, I was not especially cheerful as I set about doing the work that was to become routine during the half-year of imprisonment in this country. I put the pot of beans on the stove and made some sourdough bread. Above our beds we had put up some poles where we had placed a large quantity of dried salmon. As this food was what the dogs coveted, we had to put it up out of reach to keep them from getting into it. At first, the stench of it was sickening to me—there it was right above us as we slept. I thought that I could never learn to endure it, but surprisingly soon I discovered that I could not notice the odor of it at all. I cooked some of the fish for the dogs. First I cut it into small pieces, then boiled it all day, and finally thickened it with a little flour. During the preparation for the supper, despite my determination, I could not hold back an occasional tear that slipped out and perhaps seasoned some of the food we ate that evening.

Those first weeks brought me a multitude of impressions that were exceedingly interesting because they were so new. My husband bought three more dogs, and with the two we already had, he now possessed a fine strong team. He had obtained a financial interest in several mines that were fifteen miles away from Dawson and up the Klondike River. The mines were located on a small creek called Monte Cristo, and it was necessary for my husband to carry supplies up to his men about three times a week. On these trips up, Charlie and my husband would start very early and get back at about nine o'clock at night. These were long days for Willie and me, all alone in Dawson, knowing no one and having no place to go for amusement.

We never saw the sun anymore and it was dark practically all of the time except between twelve and one o'clock, when there was enough light in the sky to permit reading. But after and before those hours, it was necessary to keep the candle burning. We measured our candle supply and found out that we could not burn more than one a day if they were to last out the winter. To conserve our meager supply we snuffed out the light after supper and sat around the stove, opening up the front so as to let out the flickering yellow light of the flames. Of course there were no books in Dawson and except for a few precious newspapers that came through over land, there was no reading of any kind. In all probability the miners would never have read if there had been any printed matter for them. After their exhausting work they were too tired for such a mild diversion as reading, and the only satisfying relief came from going down to the saloons—absolutely the only meeting places—to chat and drink with their friends.

Everything was now completely frozen up. The river, which was our only source of water, had a crust of ice on it that was at least ten feet thick. The water holes that had been cut in this transparent layer were unique affairs, being a series of steps carved down through the ice to the running water. Every time we went for water we carried a strong ax to break the ice, which had frozen over the surface in a few minutes after the last water carrier had been there.

Now I witnessed my first real Alaskan snows, which were quite like nothing I had ever seen before. The days when the snow fell were so dark that one could not see across the space between the neighboring cabins, and so cold that we all tried to stay indoors. At the beginning of a snowstorm the flakes were very large, but as it progressed the flakes seemed to become very small and filled the air so densely that it appeared as if a great band of snow had dropped from the sky. I expected that everything would be covered many feet deep by this great white blanket, but the surprising thing was that it practically never covered the ground to a depth greater than a few feet. The snow seemed to be very dry and thin and capable of being packed down into almost no space at all. There was never any wind and consequently the snow never piled up in places and was distributed over everything evenly.

The clothing that we wore was especially made to suit this freezing climate. From head to foot one was dressed in fur. Even the face was covered by the "parkie" with only a slit for the eyes to see through. It was an odd sight to see the men on the trails with every hair of their furs standing out stiff and white with frost, and the eyebrows and lashes looking like miniature white icicles.

I soon became acquainted with our neighbor, whom I discovered to be an Indian woman married to a white man. This white man seemed to be very much devoted to his native wife— that is, when he was sober. They had a very beautiful little child—a girl—and their home life would have been happy had the man been able to keep away from liquor. He was very kind and gentle to them except during his frequent drunken sprees, and at those terrible times, all of his meanness and brutality and inhumanity would come out with ferocious energy while beating up his wife. Sitting in our cabin, sometimes alone with Willie, I would hear the crashing and smashing of furniture in our neighbor's cabin, and would shudder at the sound of her terrified shrieks, of the swish and thud of his whip, and of the wailing of the child. After he had expended all of his energy and everything had quieted down, she would always come over to me, with her torn hair and bruised body, and I would soothe her and make her a cup of hot coffee. This seldom failed to revive her spirits almost completely and she would go back to her damaged household and patch together again her nearly demolished furniture. Despite these inhuman beatings, she never seemed to hold any kind of a grudge against her husband. I discovered this to be a characteristic of the native women married to white men—they seemed to have an inordinate and unshakeable pride in their white husbands.

We came to form a close attachment to each other, this Indian woman and I, and I found much pleasure in her companionship. Occasionally she would bring me fresh moose meat or other wild game—food for kings!—which she, herself, would hunt down. Seeing that she was exceedingly proud of her little girl, I taught her how to sew for the child. Soon she had made several pretty little bonnets for the happy youngster, who when she was taken to the Squaw Dances in her fine array was the envy of all the other Indian children.

The Squaw Dances were one of the main sights and amusements at Dawson during the winter. These dances were frequented mainly by white men and their Indian women. The festivities were held in a large cabin made of logs caulked with moss. The natural festoons of moss that hung gracefully from the cracks were a most beautiful and appropriate decoration. The occasion was one of great hilarity and splendor. Boxes and crude benches ranged around the walls, and the light for the room came from candles held up by nails that were driven into a table in one corner of the room. Indian men were not admitted to this dance. The Indian women seemed to experience a gay time as they taught their half-breed children to dance the native steps, and as they themselves whirled around the room with their husbands or lovers. It was a strange sight: with the men smoking as they danced, and with the women's long hair falling over their shoulders and brown, happy faces, the place looked like a room full of dancing devils. We seldom went to these dances, for with the thermometer frequently registering sixty-five degrees below zero we found it difficult enough to keep warm in the cabin.

Once a week I would go with my husband up to the mines at Monte Cristo. To go and to return always required the entire day and much of the night. Nevertheless, I liked going better than remaining alone in Louse Town, for our cabin was situated near one of the worst saloons in town, and many terrible things happened in that place. The trails leading to the mines were very narrow and slippery, and were a highway over which hundreds of men and dog teams passed every day. The sled would slide from side to side over the icy surface, which was as slippery as glass. Frequently the men would slip and would fall heavily upon the hard ice, sometimes getting badly injured. When pulling heavy loads, the dogs would roll and fall and sometimes be struck and badly bruised by the runners of the sleds.

The Klondike mushers (this was the name given to the men who drove the dog teams carrying freight to the mines) were exceedingly brutal to their dogs, who seemed to me to be very faithful and hard-working considering the fact that they got hardly enough food to keep life in their bodies. Many times a poorly tied load would slide off of a sled, and while it was being put back on and secured, the dogs frequently would get into fights with passing dogs. Whenever a team of animals met another going in the opposite direction, both teams seemed to get in a fighting mood. At these times the mushers would whip and slash the poor beasts until their cries made me ill.

Whenever our team went up the trail, I always begged my husband to turn aside when we met another team in order to avoid these vicious scenes. In all my life I have never seen such abject cruelty as that of the mushers on the trails. In this insane striving for gold, these men seemed to lose at times all semblance of humanity when they whipped and cursed their dogs. We had learned to be kind to our own animals and never found it necessary to be brutal or to swear at them. Occasionally a slight tap of the end of the whip would more than suffice to keep them in order. The one fish a day, which was all we could afford to give them because of our dearth of food, hardly was enough to keep them alive, especially when they worked so hard. This one meal a day was given them at night before they went to sleep, for we had found that giving it to them in the morning before a day of pulling heavy loads on the trail made them sick. In order to give them all the nourishment possible, I would

Mining claim No. 2 on Bonanza Creek in the Yukon Territory, circa 1898. According to a brief article in The New York Times *on Dec. 31, 1897, William E. Knowles bought "claim No. 2, below Discovery, on the Bonanza" for $250,000.*

wash our own dishes in cold water, which I would then use to cook their fish in.

"The Forks" was a town on the trail about five miles this side of our mines, and we had to pass through it on our way. This place was the only regular town on the Klondike River, and it was the general mecca of drinking and gambling to which the tired miners flocked after their hard labors. The work in the winter was especially trying and disheartening, and the miners found a general relief and good time waiting for them in the saloons of "The Forks." Many thousands of dollars were gambled away daily in these places. Many a poor fellow would enter the saloons not thinking of gambling but only of having a good time and forgetting his tough lot, and before the evening was out would find himself penniless beside one of the gambling tables.

One did not see as much drinking as one might expect. The only place open for amusement was the saloon. The miners tried to appear happy and cheerful, but I could see trouble and often despair showing on their faces. To go into this bleak north without friends and with only hope was enough to dishearten the most cheerful and optimistic of men.

The reason for the general discouragement of the men was evident when I saw the men working in their hillside tunnels. The ground was so frozen that it was necessary to thaw it out before picking the dirt. A fire was started against the place where the earth was to be dug out, and in this way about two feet of earth could be thawed and taken out in a day. After working in this way all winter, some men would discover at the end of the season that the panning and sluicing showed hardly enough gold to pay the expenses of the year. Mining in the hills was much more difficult than working in a river bottom or on level ground. The hills were full of loose stones and gravel, which made the walls of the tunnels dangerous. The only safe way was to timber the walls and ceiling for at least ten feet into the ground.

Another difficulty and a danger to health was the continual dripping of water from the ceilings and walls. The men got very wet, cold and ill from this water. I went into one of our own tunnels and could readily see what a dismal task this mining was.

I went clear in to the far end. The walls looked very dangerous, the frozen icy ground looked almost impenetrable, and the frigid damp atmosphere with the continual rain of ice water was very uncomfortable in the extreme.

The men at the mines always welcomed us warmly. I generally made some biscuits to take to our miners, and they ate them with a joyous relish. They seemed overcome and pleased with the interest I took in them, for I was the only woman in this camp of 500 men. These miners, many of whom had wives and children in the states, seemed to ache for the sight of someone who reminded them of their own loved ones. Little Willie, the only child in the camp, was idolized. He would dance and clap his hands with joy when the men would allow him to ride into the mines on their wheelbarrows, then ride out again on top of the dirt and be dumped out along with the dirt.

CHAPTER 7

Disease

That winter typhoid fever broke out in Dawson. There was very little that could be done for those who came down with the malady because of inadequate medical supplies and assistance, so the death rate was high. Although my husband insisted that I should not expose myself, I waited until he went to the mines and then I would go from cabin to cabin doing whatever I could, cheering up the victims and relieving suffering wherever I was able. I could not stay at home when I thought of so many of those poor fellows lying alone in their tent houses and shacks with absolutely no one to give them anything to eat or drink, and they themselves too near death to tend to their own needs. It was impossible to get nurses for the sufferers. There was only one hospital in Dawson, a Catholic institution, and it was nothing more than a barn, with a medical staff composed only of men. This place of course was overflowing, and men were even lying all over the floor without receiving practically any attention or medicine. I went there only once, for my hands were full tending to those in cabins near my own home.

Efforts to help these fellows were heartbreaking, for we had to stand by frequently and watch them die for want of the simplest necessaries. The services of the doctors with medicine were too costly for most of the men, who even had to wait their turn in receiving food and drink. Vividly to this day do I remember those many thin hands that held onto mine at bedsides, and those feverish eyes that pleaded for help and comfort. When disease was upon these men, they suffered more from homesickness and want of gentle care than anything else, and I feel now that completely broken spirits took away more men that winter than typhoid fever.

One very stormy day I took a trip with my husband up to the mines, leaving Willie with my nephew at home, for it was too cold for the little fellow to make the trip. The trail was uphill most of the way, so we walked a good portion of the way so as not to fatigue the dogs. After traveling with dog teams for a while, one gets in the habit of trotting alongside or behind the sled without experiencing much fatigue. The air is so fresh and invigorating that one can go fifteen miles a day without getting very tired. When the dogs are running they seem to know just what to do, and waste no time, but if they drop into a walk they are very trying because they are so easily distracted by passing teams and always want to stop and fight.

On this trip up we visited some of my husband's old friends. These were the Berry boys—Clarence and Henry—who lived near "The Forks." These men were among the first who struck gold in the Klondike region[7], and their experience had been typical. During their first year they had worked against great odds and had nearly

7. Like the Knowles family, the Berry brothers were from Selma, California, where they farmed before they made a fortune in gold mining in the Klondike. Clarence Berry was sometimes called the "Klondike King."

starved to death. But they refused to give up and had at last struck a rich pocket of gold, which had made them the wealthiest in this region. Later I shall tell more of their mines and of riches that I saw there.

We went of course to our own claims. Our mines were located up off of the main trail and were reached by a narrow path that seemed nothing more than a sheet of ice extending up the hill. Going up I had little trouble, for someone had made steps part way up and the rest of the way I managed to scramble up by holding onto branches of trees. We turned the dogs loose at the foot of this path so that they could run and be free for a while. They always returned willingly when called.

When I started down this path matters were different. My husband went down in the way I had seen the other men do it, that was by sitting on his heels and sailing down on his feet. Then he told me to hurry, so, somewhat fearful, I sat likewise on my feet and let go. I was less fortunate: my feet suddenly came out from under me, went up in the air and got tangled up with my arms. I turned several somersaults, slid on my face, side, front and back, and finally stopped right at my husband's feet sitting up on my knees in an attitude of praying to him. A mass of mixed up snow, hair and clothing, I found myself unhurt, and waving to the men at the top who had enjoyed the whole clumsy performance, I climbed into the sled. We were whisked away down the trail as fast as the dogs could run, my husband hanging onto the gee pole and the back of the sled for his life. He was silent and I could see that he was irritated at my having taken such an unnecessary risk. When we reached home I found that I was all wet and had traveled all that distance in a very damp condition. In my tumble I had gotten a good deal of snow under my furs and, wrapped up as I was in the sled, I did not feel the dampness until I had reached home.

The following day I decided that I could no longer stand those filthy black boards that lay on the floor of the cabin, so I undertook to pry them up and turn them over. Tamped down by the feet of many years, and nearly glued together by the filth that had fallen between them, these boards required great exertion to be removed. At the end of the day, having turned over not nearly all of them, I found myself completely exhausted.

I remember that the next day I was very weak and had no appetite, and then they told me that I had typhoid fever. The food that we had was not good for one with this disease, and I became very, very sick. A friend in Dawson, a druggist, came to us and told us what to do. Will followed his instructions carefully from day to day, and I enjoyed some relief—at least a good deal more than many who were on the point of death all around in Dawson. I could see that my husband was much worried at my refusal of food and inability to go to sleep.

As I was dallying along in this way, aid suddenly came from an unexpected source. One day Henry Berry, one of the boys whose mines we had just visited, suddenly came cheerily in and coming over to my bed said, "Well, Joe, I've got something here that will put life into you," and he held up a bottle of fresh milk.

Milk in Dawson! It sounds impossible, but there it was, all ready for the drinking. The Berry boys possessed the only cow in the country, and it had been brought in from the "Outside" at a great expense. This animal cost several hundred dollars a month to feed, and a fire had to be kept going continually in her stable. When Clarence Berry had heard of my illness, he had immediately said, "Joe must have milk." So Henry had immediately hitched up his dogs, and putting the bottle of milk next to his body to keep it from freezing, he had come twenty miles to us in weather that was sixty-five degrees below zero. And not only did he come this one time but three times a week, until I was up. In all probability I would not have lived had it not been for this fresh milk, which not only revived me but also slowly brought back my appetite.

As I lay there on those poles, with my strength almost gone, my fever brought me all sorts of peculiar notions and hallucinations. One of the most amazing and persistent sensations was the thought that I had a huge pumpkin there in bed with me. With my eyes wide open, I could see it there in all of its detail. I remember now that I felt very delighted and favored by having this pumpkin, and was continually afraid that someone would come and take it away. I also hung on to a chair standing near my bed so that no one could take it away. It seemed to me that it would be very satisfying if I could lift the chair up and place it among the rafters.

The precious dishtowel was cut up for iced cloths to put on my head. My thirst was never satisfied and I would have drunk pails of water had my husband let me. I would use every ruse I could to get more water, but I was permitted only moderated draughts. My husband and nephew took turns sitting up with me at night, and I could see that this vigil was hard on them at the times when one of them would have to go up to the mines. One night I demanded that my husband and Charlie go to bed and sleep, telling them that I would be all right during the night if they put out about six cups of water to drink and put the washbasin with a large piece of ice in it for the cloths on the box beside me. Secretly I planned to drink all the water in the washbasin, no matter how dirty it might be. Assured that I would be comfortable for the night, Will looked at me seriously and said, "Joe, if you are not better by morning I'll get a doctor."

Then the men went to bed and, though planning to get up intermittently through the night, fell into a sleep of exhaustion. It was far below zero and I could hear dogs howling and moaning in the night. Very cunningly now, I began to drink the water from the cups slowly, so that it would last all night. All through the night what my husband had said about the doctor kept recurring to me, and I could actually see doctors entering the cabin every now and then in the darkness. By about one o'clock the water in the cups was gone, and I began on the washbasin, holding the ice with my thumbs and tipping the basin so that I could drink from its edge. I frequently felt the water spilling on my nightgown and getting me all wet. But I did not care—for once I was going to have enough water, at any cost.

When the water would run out, I planned to run out into the snow and get more, fatal as that would be. I had seen miners suffering from typhoid fever and if unattended, they would rush out into the snow to cool off their burning fevers. I was not thinking of consequences now, but only of relief. At about four thirty the water was all gone, and as I lay there resting and contemplating what to do next and how I could find some food, I must have dozed off to sleep.

It was not until eight o'clock that my husband awoke. The cabin was dark, the fire was out, and everything was freezing cold. When he came over to my side he could not hear me breathe, and in those frantic few moments, he later said, he thought that I was dead. But putting his hand on my face, he felt it moist, and examining close, he discovered that I was peacefully sleeping. The crisis had passed.

I slept until nine o'clock that morning, and on awakening felt so well that I decided immediately to get up. When I made the preliminary movements, however, I discovered that I was too weak to even lift my head.

The following days of convalescence were mellow and peaceful. There was no quieter cabin in Dawson. Charlie would sit with Willie on his lap telling the child stories to keep him quiet so that I could sleep. Whenever my husband went over to Dawson to tend to his affairs, my Indian neighbor would come in to tend me. She would sit on her knees by my bedside cooing like a dove in a peaceful, musical way, and the soft purr of her rising and falling croon made me want to sleep for hours.

When I was strong enough to be able to sit up, the dogs would scramble over each other and almost fight at times in order to put their heads in my lap. I had come to love them and to treat them gently. Their former masters had probably been brutal, and they seemed to understand and appreciate the difference. A woman in Dawson sent me a jar of blackberries that brought my appetite back with a rush. By the time I was well enough to get around easily, I found that the epidemic of typhoid in Dawson was waning and that there were only a few cases left in town. The number of deaths, however, had been great.

This brings me the remembrance of how those who had died were taken care of. Funeral services had been simple or nil. The question of burial was a difficult one. The ground was so solidly frozen that graves could not be dug. As a result, the corpses were placed as they were in a special cabin and left there until spring, when ground could be thawed out for them, or they could be sent to the "Outside." The "dead" cabin was within half a block from our own cabin. One time I went there and peeked in, as usual a victim of my funereal curiosity, and got a good shiver when I saw about two dozen bodies in there stacked up like cords of wood.

Those of us who were new in the Klondike longed for spring to come, as the dark, depressing, stormy days were getting on our nerves. The family with the other little boy who had come up on the boat with us from San Francisco lived ten miles up the Klondike. The woman had not been strong, and whenever I had gone to see her, I found her nervous, depressed, homesick and ill. Her husband had come into Dawson to do engineering work, but had become discouraged and downhearted at his wife's sickness. I found this same trouble with most of the women who had come in—they would almost die from homesickness. They were snow- and ice-bound here, and could not possibly go to the "Outside" except by traveling over the most dangerous of frozen country. Anyone who attempted to go home to the States during the winter cared little for his life.

Willie and I came to find it very interesting to go into the center of Dawson and see the sights. At times we would almost freeze as we stood in the cold watching the strange sights of the fur-covered human beings trudging along the streets and stumbling in and out of saloons and stores. These stores were unlike any retail stores I had ever seen before. They were made of logs, with one door and two windows. Inside there were no floors, and the ground was covered with sawdust, which helped to keep the places warmer. Hanging from pegs, hooks, and strings were the goods which one was to buy, or perhaps what one wanted could be found piled up with a lot of other things in some corner. Boots, skis, snowshoes, sleds, fur parkies, mutlock[8] boots, and other clothing were hung up or strewn all over the place.

When one entered one of these places, one found the lights so dim that he could see nothing. Soon he could discern a red-hot stove over in one dusky corner where there would be a number of miners telling stories, or laying unconscious, sleeping or drunk. If one were not careful, he would probably step on several dogs that lay all over the floors sleeping. The air was filled with tobacco smoke, which made everything dim and misty. Everyone who came here desired either to lounge around or to buy whiskey or tobacco, or perhaps, and this was seldom, to buy clothing and food. Most of the food was brought in by the miner himself. Yet food could be purchased. Eggs that looked like coarse meal and evaporated potatoes resembling rolled oats were mainly used in Alaska. Butter and milk also came in five-gallon cans.

In the streets one might have thought that he were among wild animals. The men coming in from the mines looked like huge bears walking on their hind feet. Their faces were necessarily covered by their parkies and nosepieces, and one could see eyes fringed with frosted brows and lashes. The parkie was a huge piece of fur that covered the whole upper part of the body and reached down to the knees. A hood, which covered the head, had a foxtail on it that almost completely covered the face. This was an Indian garment, which was so effective in warding off the cold that one seldom could freeze if properly dressed in it. Everyone wore long fur boots, with the fur on the outside, in which people's feet seldom got cold.

Anyone properly equipped with food and clothing did not find it very hard in Dawson. There was a great demand for labor.

---

8. Typically known as mukluk boots.

Men crossing frozen Crater Lake, British Columbia, in 1898 using sleds outfitted with sails.

The common laborer got ten dollars a day mushing and draying, and fifteen if he owned his own sleigh—huge wages in those days. This was the hardest work one could do, and it was very trying. It was said that even the "goody men," that is, the strictly religious, would say bad words that they would not want their friends on the "Outside" to have heard. When on the trails, which were as slippery and smooth as glass, the dogs would get to fighting, and its was necessary to untangle a mass of fighting dogs and harnesses frozen stiff in the icy temperature. It was impossible to ride on the back of a sled for any considerable distance without something happening in the way of falls, fights, slips, or tip-overs.

One night we heard a terrible cry coming up from the river. My husband dressed quickly and ran outdoors to see if he could locate the person in trouble. In the distance he heard some drunken men laughing and talking loud, and after looking around and listening for a while, he concluded that these men had made the noise during their revels, so he came back to bed. The next morning the City Engineer was found dead at the river right near to our cabin. The evidence showed that on his way home from "The Forks," he had decided to take a shortcut across the river. He had fallen into a hole cut in the ice by some negligent person who had forgotten to cover it up. The hole had been very small and the ice not so thick because of the swiftness of the river here. In falling he had the presence of mind to throw out his arms so that he did not fall through; but he could not pull himself out. Around him on the ice were great scratches that showed how he had struggled. Realizing, apparently, that in a few moments he would be lifeless, he had taken some valuable papers from his pockets. There they were lying as far away from him as he could push them. This whole thing was especially unfortunate because we felt that we could have saved him if those yelling, drunken men had not deceived us in the night.

Freezing part of one's body was a great danger all of the time, and would often occur accidentally. I recall many poor men who had had their feet or hands so badly frozen that the doctors were compelled to amputate them. Narrow escapes taught us to be cautious.

We had always difficulty in inducing Charlie, my nephew, to wear his fur coat. This worried my husband, who feared that the boy might go farther from home than he expected and freeze to death. One morning I heard my husband urging Charlie to wear his coat when he went across the river to get wood for us, but the boy thought it unnecessary. It was exceedingly cold and a bad storm was coming up. When he came in with his wood, we all noticed a large white spot on his wrist, but the significance of it did not occur to us at the time. After he had been in the warm cabin for a short time, he suddenly began to complain of a sharp pain in his arm. Immediately we rushed out and grabbed some snow, which we applied continuously to his wrist. Luckily, the pain went away soon, but the trouble did not cease with the pain, for nearly all winter he had a bad looking sore on his wrist, which looked and acted like a burn, but which healed only gradually. The boy wore all of his furs after that experience.

The Indian woman, my neighbor, came to me one day, and in her broken way, told me that she and her husband were going to the "Outside" to visit her husband's people. He had not seen them for forty years, and was now so anxious to leave that he decided to go out over land despite the dangers that this trip involved. But what worried the Indian wife was not at all the trip, but leaving her home for the first time and visiting these strange white people, whom she was afraid would not treat her kindly. She was happy to go in one respect, for she knew that a white man generally, almost inevitably, left forever his squaw wife and children when he went to the "Outside."

I advised her to wear her furs and all of her native garments until she arrived at his home, for I thought that this might greatly impress his folks. When she was preparing to leave she asked me, with a great deal of pride, if I would like to take a ride in her new sleigh and dog team, which her husband had just purchased for her. Knowing that the Indians value more than anything else their sleighs, just as we do our fine automobiles, I accepted, though I was somewhat afraid that she might not know how to drive the team.

Soon she arrived at the door and proudly displayed her new sled, all lined with bright red flannels and heavy furs, drawn by six malamute dogs, arrayed in shiny new harnesses. The lead dog carried a string of little bells, which jingled joyously in the snow.

She had the dogs standing in a row, and cracked her whip over the head of any animal that made as if to lie down. By the way she cracked her whip, I knew that she understood how to "mush."

After she had covered Willie and me all up with robes and furs, leaving just enough room to peek out, she jumped onto the back of the sled, grabbed the gee pole that guided us, and cracked her whip over the dogs' heads. We heard them yelp and off we all went! It seemed as if we swept through the newly fallen snow like a gale, with snow flying in every direction. It was a crisp wintry day, and we were enjoying the dusky beauty of the scene as we rushed up the Klondike trail. We had gone about a mile when suddenly the dogs saw a rabbit, or imagined they did, and we whizzed over an embankment and turned over and over as we went down the other side. As Willie and I were rolled up so tight in our blankets, we went with the sled, the dogs and all, rolling over and over until we reached the bottom of the hill.

When we dragged ourselves out and found ourselves unhurt, I laughed at the whole thing, but the look on the face of my friend was one of dismay, disappointment, and then anger at the dogs. Her pride had been damaged, and she was angrily quiet as she jerked the dogs up the hill, untangled the harness, arranged the sled, and packed us back in. She had said not a word and I knew we were in for a wild ride. Back over the main trail we flew, and I could hear the whip constantly sing over my head and snap angrily over the dogs, who, though it did not touch them, yelped madly. Through the streets we dashed, with everyone turning around wondering why the rush. Had we struck a stump or the corner of a cabin there would have been a disaster. Right up to our cabin we flew, and with beating hearts that had stood still several times, we crept out of our robes. She did not say a word when we thanked her for our wonderful ride, but jumped back onto the sled and cracking the whip went tearing away, with her parkie hood fallen off and her black hair flying beautifully behind her. Her ride had been a failure for her! Not, however, for us. She never mentioned the ride afterwards.

The dreary days of winter became very oppressive there in that gloomy cabin in Louse Town. Every day began by putting on the fish to cook for the dogs, and preparing the apples and the pot of pork and beans for us. The atmosphere of the place became rank with the odor of this cooking and of a thousand and one other smells, and airing the place out was impossible with the temperature outside many degrees below zero. Although most people turned their dogs loose outside when they were not being used, I could not permit our animals to be used this way, and always left them in the cabin with us. These poor animals, half-famished on the fish-a-day diet, would stand with their heads resting on the bed looking upward at the fish, which lay on the poles above them.

There were practically no families in Dawson that I could visit. Occasionally my husband and I would go to some of the stores and listen to the miners telling of their adventures. Most of their tales were of their first hardships in Dawson, of how they almost died of starvation with only beans to live on and the chance of trapping wild game. They would tell of how they kept warm by skinning the wild animals they succeeded in capturing, and getting the Indian women to make garments from them. In those earlier days of which they spoke, the hills and mountains immediately around Dawson were covered with large trees, but now all of these had been cut down, leaving only scraggy bushes and small trees. In the dusk when the snow was on the mountains, these black stumps and poles would look like men marching along the side of the mountain. There was no longer any wild game except small creatures in these hills, for they had all been hunted out or scared away by this time.

It was on one of these monotonous days that through our door came a man who had not taken the trouble even to knock. Miners ordinarily did not knock when they entered their friend's cabin, but as this man had not expected to see a woman and child here, he seemed a little abashed at first. My husband told him that we were just sitting down for lunch, and that he was welcome if he wished to join us. A box was placed next to Willie, and the man sat down. We were having a treat for that meal—moose meat, precious fresh meat that an Indian had captured in the hills. I now noticed that the man, whom my husband was acquainted with, had been drinking and did not seem under good control. While Willie was eating, he accidentally let his plate slip into his lap and his meat fell onto the floor. For some unknown reason, this man leaned over and grabbing Willie by the head with one hand, lifted the meat from the floor with the other, and began stuffing it down the child's throat. In a second my husband had jumped over the table and with his hand on the man's neck, went into the corner with him. The table was upset and the dogs immediately pounced upon the meat, devouring it instantly. When the men rose, the outsider looked abashed and crestfallen.

My husband noticed for the first time that the man was drunk, and felt rather ashamed for treating him so roughly. He then took the man home, fearing that he might otherwise fall down and thus freeze to death. While they were gone I was somewhat fearful for my husband's safety, for this man was notorious as a hard character and was reputed for shooting on the instant. Several days later this man came around and apologized to me for his actions, a courtesy that surprised me.

CHAPTER 8

Slumming in Dawson

There was great excitement and bustle in town one day when an Indian guide brought news that a sleigh full of mail was coming in over the snows from the "Outside" and would soon arrive. As soon as this information went around, the trails into Dawson became alive with miners who, long hungry for news from their folks at home, dropped their tools immediately and started for town. My husband came in from his mines in the evening and said that the trails down the Klondike were lined with howling and fighting dog teams, and that he was nearly sick from hearing the swearing of men and the whipping of dogs.

After we had thawed him out and filled him with a supper of beans, applesauce and sourdough bread, he proposed that we go into the town and visit some of the saloons. Things would be going at full blast tonight, he said, and I would see high-life in Dawson that I might not ever have another chance to see. I had of course not been in any of the saloons, and was rather afraid of the venture, but my husband insisted.

The thermometer told us that it was sixty-four degrees below zero. At about nine o'clock we hitched up our team and started out. The streets were nearly deserted, for the cold and the hilarity of the day had sent all the men into the saloons, where we could hear dancing, drinking, and gambling going on at full speed. Occasionally we would see belated travelers coming in from the mines, driving their dogs hurriedly forward. The air was full with a perfect din of howling, which sounded as if every dog team in Alaska had been brought into Dawson and turned loose. The ill temper and profanity I heard whenever we met a team made me think that gentleness and kindness had long since deserted this country.

We finally came to the "Klondike," a large dance hall and saloon where my husband thought I could see all the typical sights that make up amusement for the miners. My husband went to inquire of the proprietor how he could get me in without being seen or molested. When he returned he told me to follow him around to the back of the building. Feeling a little frightened, I got out of the sled and pushed and pulled myself through the snow until I came to a place in the rear of the building where I could see a ladder that led up and into a window about fifteen feet from the ground.

Steam had come through the eaves back here, and great icicles reached all the way from the roof, high up, down to the snow. The ladder itself was ice-covered and looked dangerous, but with a little persuasion I followed my husband up the shaky steps to the window, which the proprietor had kindly left open for us. My husband grabbed me in his open arms and pulled me in. I confess that I felt abashed and ashamed for entering in this fashion.

We found ourselves in a narrow hall. At the far end was a flickering candle, which gave out a faint and ghostly light in this narrow passage. Down below us and to one side, we could hear shouting, laughing, and dancing. Feeling my way behind my husband down this dingy hall, I followed him into a "box," where we locked ourselves in. There was a window in front of us, and I timidly peeked out of it. Below me I saw the high-life, or rather, the low-life of Dawson in all of its glory. There were curtains on the window, and we drew them together sufficiently so that we would not attract attention. We sat right up next to the window so that we could see everything, and with our parkies drawn up around our faces, we attracted some attention as being strangers, but no one suspected that there was a woman in our party. Occasionally men would gaze up at our box with questioning looks on their faces, and several times someone tried to open our door, but went away when they found it locked.

The room right below us was at first so full of tobacco smoke that I was stifled and almost had to leave. As the dancing progressed, however, the air cleared up somewhat. I felt better and could see the scene below more clearly. Part of the floor was roped off for the dancers, who were whirling around apparently in great enjoyment. They did not make much noise, for the men were wearing fur boots. The women wore very short skirts, and with their comely faces, mostly painted, they looked pretty and enticing as they danced. I may say that the dancing was no more indecent than much of what I have seen in later days in our large cities.

Sawdust covered the floor outside of the roped-in areas. To one side were the gambling tables and roulette wheels, around which a crowd of men and women were gathered with tense, interested expressions on their faces. In the center of the tables were stacked small bags of gold dust, amounting probably to many thousands of dollars. When one saw those eager little groups of men and women, most of them smoking and peering at the gold bags and cards and chips, with the single candle in the middle of the table throwing moving shadows over their faces, one could almost imagine that he was looking down into some cavern in Hades.

Large quantities of whiskey, wine, and beer were being dispensed over a rough board bar, behind which stood large casks of the sparkling liquids. As the evening progressed, the effect of the alcohol began to become more noticeable and the dark corners and sides of the room began to fill up with sleeping, drunken men who had unceremoniously lain down flat on the floor. I could not find it within me to condemn these people, because their jobs were too disheartening and inhuman for any person, and their own cabins, which were cold and dismal, offered no relief from their rigorous labors. I knew that most of these men who were dancing here and became drunken and sodden were really good, kindly men who could find no other place to go for warmth and cheer.

The great attraction for the evening was a play that was staged on a crude platform at one end of the room. The actors and actresses were of a degraded sort, and took special delight in telling vulgar stories, which were received by the audience with great enthusiasm. The play itself was not as bad as I have seen in good theatres at home; we were in fact surprised that the performers showed a certain amount of dramatic skill. It was a wild western affair, and I remember a lot of rough fighting and talking. The play ended in a great "bloody" fight between two men. The squabble seemed to be over a woman, who in the course of the combat had all of her clothing stripped off. Then she was "killed," and peace was thus restored between the combatants, who in concerted action cut the body in half by some sort of sleight-of-hand trick. The action was mainly burlesque, and considerably realistic in parts, especially when the woman was dissected.

Even way up in this remote land, the Salvation Army was at work ministering to the unfortunates. There down below us was a woman in the Salvation Army uniform. She was going about, not preaching, but talking amiably with various people, and ready to help anyone whom she could. There were several of these women in Dawson, and they were highly respected even by the worst of men and women.

Across the room and up in the box opposite us, I could see several men and women talking hilariously, and by the amount of liquor they were consuming, it was evident that before long they would be helplessly drunk. By midnight, practically everyone was badly intoxicated, and we concluded that it was time to leave. I refused to go down that treacherous ladder, so we decided to make a rush downstairs and out the front door. Unlocking the door of our box, we walked quickly out and down the creaking stairs. As we made our way through the milling crowd of people, I caught sight of a number of drunken men and women pawing at each other in a stupid way. I saw bleary eyes, gaping mouths, and staggering forms, and the picture of these things remains very vivid in my memory. Though the fresh air outside nearly froze my lungs, it seemed, our trip home in the sled was a great relief, both physically and mentally.

Perhaps my anxiety about being molested there was unfounded to a degree. Nevertheless, any woman found in a Dawson saloon was classed with all the rest. There were certain things in Dawson that stamped a woman as bad: one was the chewing of gum; another was dancing inside the ropes in a saloon and being seen in such a public place. It was not so much in the saloons, however, that immorality took place. Behind the main street of Dawson was a row of log cabins, which were the headquarters of these underworld women, a rather varied crowd of riff-raff, with representatives from practically every race and nationality. Each woman had a small cabin about eight by ten feet square, with a small window and a door at the front. In one end of each place was generally a box that served as a dresser. It was here, generally before the open window, that each morning the occupant of the room took her morning dip from a small tin washbasin.

Many of the trails leading from the mines passed by the windows of these places. No man could get by them without being accosted by these women with a flood of obscene remarks, and they would almost pull the men into their dens. There were no lights on this street, but at night one could easily distinguish it at a distance by the row of lights in the windows, which looked like winking stars.

Up one of the creeks near Dawson, there was another and smaller collection of these women who were of a better sort. Mainly they had been good women who had come into Dawson hoping to make easy money by serving doughnuts and coffee to men that passed on the trails. They tried to live properly at first, but generally finding no cabin or tent to accommodate them, and becoming ill and sadly disillusioned, they would begin to frequent the saloons, where their downfall was assured. There were many men who would gladly give them a home, and frequently there were marriages. A few kind and sympathetic men, without asking any questions about their past character, would take in these down-and-outers, and when spring would come, would send them to the "Outside."

Women stand in front of a row of houses in Louse Town, circa 1899.

Drinking, gambling, and the other irregularities did not seem especially evil way up here in the North, in this sun-less, gloomy, and lonely place. It was natural and forgivable for these men and women to give themselves over to anything that they could find cheer and comfort in.

Many of these creatures were compelled to enter this sort of life. While I was in Dawson, I personally made the acquaintance and soon became a good friend of one of these women. She lived in a cabin not far from us, and I made many visits to see and comfort her. She and her two small children had come into Dawson alone, hoping to establish a restaurant. But the sickness of her children and of herself soon left her destitute. Suddenly I noticed a man around her place, and I soon discovered that he was staying there.

Evidently she had been driven to receive this sort of aid. Several months later the man disappeared, and another soon took his place.

It was when she came down with typhoid fever that I began to visit her regularly, and I found that she was a good, well-meaning woman who apparently had no other course open to her than the one she was following. Later, when I went up to the mines, the Salvation Army women looked after her.

CHAPTER 9

Hardships at the Mines

The Christmas of that year we probably had the only pie in Dawson. Though I had to make the crust from bacon grease, and the filler with humble dried apples, to our palates it was a delicacy for kings. The rest of our Christmas dinner was set up in as gorgeous a style: there was fresh stew with dumplings (dishes that were unheard of in this country), and beans, and potatoes made into balls, and applesauce.

On the afternoon of Christmas day, my Indian friend came over to see me. I gave her a little breast pin, which I had always worn. This delighted her so much that she stood before my small mirror for many minutes admiring herself from every possible angle. In a short while, she left the mirror and went home without saying a word. When I moved aside the box where she had been seated, I was surprised to find a small box of candy and also a queer little cushion made from bed ticking, with some grotesque designs on top made from beadwork. The candy, I knew, cost my friend considerable money, for sweets were scarce in Dawson.

There were few days as pleasurable as Christmas, and the days that followed were monotonous and difficult. Right behind our cabin was the worst saloon in Louse Town, an establishment that ran day and night. Whenever my husband was away, I kept the doors barred, and luckily, too, for several times I had drunken men come to the door and try to get in. Some men would get into such drunken frenzies that they would strip off their clothes for some insane reason and run out of the saloon into the snow; they would be immediately pursued by friends, and a great commotion would result, with the air filled with foul language as the drunk was escorted back to his clothes.

I did not have Charlie with me now, for my nephew was working as a day laborer at the Dominion mining camp about 20 miles away. He was working every day, receiving 10 to 15 dollars for his hire, and was able to visit us about once a month. I believe that it would frighten almost any woman at times to be left alone with a child of four years under these conditions.

We lived on the main trail that led directly into Dawson, and the important branch that led up the Klondike River forked off right in front of our cabin. When the dog teams arrived at this fork, they frequently did not know in what direction to go. Many of the mushers would beat and whip the poor animals until they would almost drop from pain and fright. This inhumanity was so agonizing to me that at times when I would hear a dog team coming, I would go outside and wait for it to pass, hoping that the men would not beat the animals in my presence. My husband told me that this always made them furious. I did not care, and I know that if I had been a man, I would have probably been all scarred up trying to prevent some of these beatings. I think I suffered more from these experiences than from any other hardships in Alaska. Whippings did not seem to affect the malamutes very much, for immediately afterward they would jump around in joy and their little eyes would shine with playfulness if one talked to them. But the "Outside" dogs, most of them the most faithful and trusting creatures, would seem completely crestfallen and unhappy after such abuse. If I had an opportunity, I would sometimes go to them and put my arms around their necks. They were never savage and would respond immediately to a little affection. Maltreatment was so unnecessary!

One night my husband came home so late from his trip to the mines that for a while I thought he would not possibly return at this late hour. He had taken an especially heavy load of provisions up to the mines and this had necessitated walking most of the way. Of course this meant several bad falls on the slippery trails, those sudden falls in which his feet would unexpectedly go out from under him, causing him to fall heavily on his back or side on that hard ice. These falls were very weakening and frequently made men seriously ill.

When my husband entered, he jerked off his frozen parkie and said huskily: "I'll be damned if I'll go up that trail again, even if it results in my starving." And he gave his parkie a kick that sent it under the bed like a shot.

Though I laughed at his mood, I knew that he was serious, and that something was about to "break." I thawed him out, as usual, with a hot supper, and then stood ready to hear what was coming. As we were around the stove, he suddenly broke his continued silence:

"Joe, how would you like to go up to the claims to live? Don't you think we could manage very well in one of those small cabins there? I'm through with making these trips."

I was more than glad to go any place where I would not be so much alone as in Dawson, and was ready to start right away. I knew that he was starting several new tunnels and that it would be very desirable for him to be on the job all the time. Our new home would not be more than ten feet square, with one paneless window and a door so low that we would have to stoop when entering. We planned to go the very next day.

The next morning I asked my Indian friend, who had not yet left for the "Outside," to assist me in packing my things. She seemed to feel badly about our moving, and expressed it by not saying a word while she packed. Like the other natives, she knew how to pack everything so that if the sled tipped over nothing would fall out or slip off. When she had finished, she had left a place for Willie, whom she rolled up into a cocoon-like ball and tied onto the sled in her own Indian fashion. Then she turned and ran to her cabin as fast as she could, without making any sign of good-bye. I went after her, of course, to wish her well, for I would probably never see her again. But I found her cabin door locked. Thus do these Indians hate to display their emotions! She was a very human little creature.

The weather was so cold that the moisture from our breath froze immediately when it came into the air, and fell in feathery mists at our feet. We decided to take our time in order to avoid accidents of any kind. About half way up, we came to a part of the trail where a man had constructed a bridge and charged a toll for passing over it. The toll-taker was surprised to see a woman on such a frigid day, and insisted in having me enter and be warmed up by the fire and a hot cup of coffee. The man went out with my husband to weigh our sled. I heard Will say that he would not pay for fifty pounds of the load. I stepped to the door. The man seemed surprised and was about to make some sort of retort, when my husband said: "Come here!"

Then he opened a robe and showed little Willie all snug and warm. I was surprised at the man's response. He threw up his hands and said, "My God," and immediately unhitched the dogs and pulled the whole sled into the cabin. Then with a most gentle and beaming expression on his face, he lifted Willie out, and placing him on his lap began to feed the child something warm. And then he told us that he had left just a little boy on the "Outside." With tears on his cheeks, he talked on about his little boy and family. He insisted that he give us his bed for the night, that we be his guests. I could see that the sight of Willie had made the poor fellow badly homesick.

But we had to go on, with a promise from the toll-keeper that he would come to see us frequently at the mines. At about eight o'clock in the evening we turned up the hill to our claims, nearly frozen. Right ahead of us were the lights of cabins, and they seemed to twinkle as a welcome to us.

A Mr. St. George stopped us at his cabin and said we could rest there until we could fix up our own little home. After a hot meal, my husband went ahead to unload our goods at our own place. A short time later, I skipped over to see what our new home looked like.

I opened the door of our little nine-by-eleven-foot home with some misgivings. But they were all dispelled when I saw

A dog team arriving at mining claim No. 2 below Bonanza Creek with a load of lumber, circa 1899.

everything very cute and home-like. My husband had unpacked all of our things, scraped the ice off of the walls and pole floor, and had built a crackling fire on which beans and apples were cooking merrily. After the stove had been put up, there hardly seemed room for anything else. What a cramped up place it was, and yet, how homey!

We brewed a pot of coffee and then, oblivious to all the many inconveniences we were to have here, we prepared our bed, which was to be a fur robe on hard poles, with a blanket and robe over us. I had been living so close to a noisy saloon so long that I could not sleep at first in this quiet place, where only the dismal wail of a dog interrupted the still night.

This little cabin was to be our home until we left, and I came to love it, humble and mean as it was. Whenever I had company, I almost had to put them to bed in order to have enough room in which to make the meals. The best idea that one can get of this cabin can be taken from the first words that Willie uttered the next morning, when he saw it for the first time, having spent the night with Mr. St. George:

"Mama, why, you can make breakfast while you are laying in bed, can't you?"

The men in the gulch here did not like the idea of a woman coming into their midst. Here I was the only woman in a camp of 500 rough miners! They had it all figured out that the first thing I would do would be to interfere with their gambling and good times. I realized this and decided never to make any sign that I disapproved of some of their actions, never to moralize or to interfere in any way. I came to know most of them, and helped them in several ways. Few of them knew how to cook their food so that it was fit to eat, with a consequence that there was a good deal of sickness around. Soon I had taught many of them how to cook their bread and their other grub so that it was palatable, and would myself prepare some delicacies, which I brought to the sick men.

Wherever I could, I ministered by my own remedies, because a doctor could be brought up from Dawson only at the exorbitant price of $150. We had brought a large quantity of simple medicines— quinine, salts, and the like—and these remedies seemed in most cases to be entirely sufficient. At one time, there was an epidemic of mumps that swept through the camps. After about a month of working as a friend among the miners, all the feeling of suspicion with which they had at first looked at me seemed to have gone.

A view of Bonanza Creek, circa 1900.

The window in our cabin was like everybody else's, without panes, and the canvas that we tacked over it did not keep out the freezing temperatures. My husband took a bundle of photograph plates, which I had found in the old Indian cabin in Dawson, and made a window for us that had eighteen panes in it. This gorgeous window filled everyone who saw it with wonder and awe, and it was regarded as a thing of rare beauty and utility. We had as many panes of glass in our window as there probably were in the whole town of Dawson.

All around us was a treeless and gray waste. All the large trees had been cut to make cabins, and all that was left were scrubby bushes. Fires had swept through this country during the summer, leaving only black stumps that looked grim and lifeless in the

A large crowd of men, along with some women and children, wait for the mail at the Dawson City post office.

snow. It was necessary to go a long ways up the mountain to get wood to burn.

The miners who did not give themselves to dissipation were really heroes to endure these murky conditions, to tolerate these dreary days of agony of muscle, and of empty rest periods; especially when they had families on the "Outside," the thoughts of long separation ought to have made them despair. Knowing that I was a good woman, one man came to me one day with a hopeless look on his face:

"Mrs. Knowles, what will I do? I can't go on in this cheerless, Godless way. I have a wife and children at home who are continually in my mind, and it's against all my principles to betray them, to go in for all this high-life with the rest of the boys. But, my heavens, this solitude, this loneliness is too much to ask of any man. You don't know how terrible it is to see the boys leave for "The Forks" or for Dawson for a good time in the saloons and with the women while I must stay here in a cold, depressing cabin. I don't know what to do!"

His case was like that of many others, and as far as I could see there was no way out for him. I consoled and comforted him as best I could, and felt deeply sorry for him when he left. There was no entertainment for these men besides dissipation. Once in a very long while, someone coming in overland to Dawson would bring a newspaper, and this would be passed around and read so many times that it would soon be in worn tatters.

The mail came in to the mining district twice throughout these eight months of winter. I remember that I went down into Dawson one of these times, hoping to get a letter from my family. In front of the crude Post Office was a long line of men, in which some men had stood for days, hoping that something might turn up for them. This line moved so slowly that a special entrance for women was made through the back way, so that they would not have trouble with the men and would not have to stand out in that long line during the freezing weather.

There was no news for me, however, and disappointed as I was, I was determined not to worry about my girls. I knew that they had written, but that the letters had not come through. Getting mail through the ice-bound wastes was a precarious job. Several times the winter boats that brought the mail to Dyea were wrecked and the mail lost. Sleds carrying mail over the snows would sometimes crash through the ice, resulting in the letters becoming wet and encased in ice. When they were delivered in Dawson, they had to be thawed out before the anxious men could read the news, provided the ink had not been smeared by the water.

I have seen some men cry like babies when reading their letters, whether the news was good or bad, and most would be so overjoyed that they would pass their letters around. And then there were others who received nothing, and then their spirits would be black. In all the time that I was in the Klondike, I heard not a word from my family, though they later told me that they had written. I consoled myself by remembering that before I came to Dawson I had been warned by my husband that I might not hear a word from home, and also that if I did hear from home the news might be bad. The men at the gulch often brought me their letters to read, and would talk of their home and families as if I personally knew them all.

The time went by much more quickly at the gulch because I was not left alone so much there. My husband seldom went to Dawson and when he did, I went with him. We left Willie with St. George and the other miners; the men were so fond of playing and talking with the child, probably seeing in him their own children, that they would lay off of their work to take care of him while we were gone.

Willie soon became a regular "musher" and learned to crack his whip with skill. Whenever he accidentally struck one of the dogs, he would stop the whole team and rush up to the offended animal, put his arm around its neck, and tell it he was awful sorry and would not do it again. The men taught him to jump onto the back of the sled while it was going, and the boy was therefore completely convinced that he was in every respect now a man.

It may be a question in many people's minds as to how we did our washing. Except for collars and socks, we did not wash our clothes. To immerse things in water and to hang them out to dry would have meant bringing them in as pieces of ice. As a result I merely put the things out into the snow, in that terrible cold, and when they were brought in later, we would find them smelling sweet and clean. We had practically nothing to change into, but the few robes and furs we had were cleansed in this way. Such luxuries as sheets and pillowcases were unknown in the Klondike.

One evening my husband came in from the mine and complained that his head was throbbing with pain. Immediately I put him to bed, prepared a hot drink for him, and put a mustard plaster on his chest. All that night his fever was frightfully high, and his condition was even worse in the morning, when he murmured that the pain in his lungs was awful. It was evident that he had pneumonia. The possibility of getting a doctor up here was nearly out of the question, and as I had already tended one man at the gulch who had suffered from this direful disease, I decided to nurse and minister to him myself. I felt confident that I could do as well as the doctors who were in Dawson.

Mr. St. George asked to take care of Willie for me, and I prepared myself for a long vigil and fight with this terrible disease. What if the results would be fatal! For many nights I sat there watching him in the ups and downs of this disease, and during the days I would do some quiet cooking, and perhaps snatch a few hours sleep by his side. He slept most of the time, but seemed to be consumed most of the time by a torrid fever.

Our wood supply was fast dwindling, and I knew that we would soon be out. Knowing that the miners had a difficult time themselves procuring their wood, I could not persuade myself to ask any of the men to help me out. Many of them came in during the daytime to ask about the sick man, and it was evident that his lingering illness troubled them. As the invalid slept, and as his fever made him intensely hot, I knew that the cold would not bother him, especially as I kept him wrapped well in furs.

I decided to put out the fire when it was not urgently needed. I conserved wood for some time this way, but it soon became evident that one day I would have to go up to the mountains myself to get more wood. One night, after letting the fire go long enough to heat the plasters, I wrapped a fur robe about me and let the fire go out. When morning came, I prepared to set out for wood, and at about seven o'clock harnessed the dogs for that purpose. Then I opened the door very quietly so as not to wake my husband. There before me the miners had piled wood so high that I could hardly see out of the doorway! They had left a place for me to slip through, and there right outside was a huge tub of clean snow for water, and beside it was a kettle of cooked beans that were frozen and needed only to be thawed out for breakfast. The miners had apparently followed closely my needs, for the wood was cut in the proper length for the stove, and the beans cooked so that I would not have the moisture and smoke from my own cooking.

The kindness of these rough men was my only solace in these trying days when death might have come into our household at any time. The attention which these men showed acted, I believe, as a sort of balm to my husband's morale, and encouraged him to get well. Whenever they would go to Dawson, they returned with some special tasty food for my husband. When he was at his lowest they brought in warm food for several days, so that I would have nothing to do but watch him.

One night he became very restless, and I felt deeply worried. To conserve the wood, I had let the fire go out, and in that cold cabin, with only a fur robe around me, I felt at the end of my rope. It seemed that all of this care was useless and there was no hope left. As I sat there in a sort of despondent daze, I suddenly saw him rise from his bed and walk right past me and through the door to the freezing cold outside. I must have fainted, for I found myself lying on the floor, wondering what had happened. Looking up I saw my husband sleeping peacefully on the bed, and rushing to him, I found him sleeping in the calmest and quietest manner. I could tell by his placid countenance and breathing that the climax had been passed! My vision of him going out the door had been the result, probably, of my exhausted and distressed state of mind.

I could hardly wait until morning. Then, when I could first go out, I ran down the hill with all my might to St. George's cabin. Flinging the door open without knocking, I grabbed Willie up from the floor where he was playing and rushed back to our cabin without saying a word to anyone. This was due partly to my ecstasy and partly to the fear that my husband would want to get up.

St. George rushed over after me, wondering what had happened. Later he and some of the men who had seen my dash down the hill said they knew by it that the danger was over. All that morning I whistled and sang, wanting within me to both cry and scream at the same time. The soft snow never looked purer or whiter, nor the scanty foliage on the brush more beautiful. It was then that the men told me that they had considered the condition of my husband especially serious, and that they had been contemplating carrying him down to Dawson, and if necessary to the "Outside."

My husband gained his strength very rapidly now. The miners frequently dropped in with some morsels that would help a sick man feel better, and such morsels were hard to get. St. George went clear to Dawson one day, and returned with a good piece of moose meat. When he brought this in and placed it on the table, all the care and hardship seemed to drop off of our shoulders, and in place came a moving appreciation of the sympathy and kindness of these noble men.

CHAPTER 10

Spring Drives Away the Darkness

One dark, bitter-cold night, my husband came hurriedly into the cabin and exclaimed: "Come outside! I have never seen the northern lights more beautiful!"

We threw on our robes hastily, ran outdoors and found a place where we could lay down, for looking upward would become quickly tiring. After we got settled for the sight, we waited and waited, yet no lights. The sky seemed to be far away, the stars appearing dim and faint. The cold crept through our furs and seemed to penetrate to our very bones, and the moisture from our breath froze quickly as it came out of the holes in our hoods.

We had just about decided that the show was off for the night, when the whole sky—east, west, north, and south—burst into one great flare of flaming clouds. For a moment the clouds remained motionless; then, they began to roll and tumble together upwards toward the top of the sky. As if some unseen god were throwing noiseless thunderbolts, long streamers of fire burst from these clouds, and assuming flaring, gorgeous colors, they shot across the sky from horizon to horizon.

As quick as a thought, the streamers now changed into myriads of plumes, in fantastic shapes that dazzled us. They seemed to float on the sky as if some mighty wind were wafting them about. High up in the zenith, a sun now seemed to be shining, but only for a moment, for all these shapes appeared like rolls of fleecy lamb's wool. As we watched the mass of flaming fleece, from which shot brilliant beams of colored lights, the whole sky became suddenly black, and we lay there on the ground as if stunned by those wonders.

The aurora did not appear every night, but only when the temperature was very low, and the atmosphere uncommonly clear. It was a sight so wondrous as to be indescribable by anyone; a pen-picture can give really no satisfactory notion of its splendor. It is strange that in this ghostly, unbeautiful land, one should find this, the most beautiful of natural phenomena.

Such beauties and compensations in our sordid life at the gulch were few. The claims which we held were not rich. We had divided them into five sections, each of which we had rented out a miner, who received the largest percentage of what he mined. Such tunnels as these generally had to be worked for the whole winter and following summer before the miner found out whether the property was worth anything.

Hundreds of men worked all of this time and found that they had been working in worthless ground; then they would start for the "Outside," penniless and completely broken down in health and spirit. But there were others, and they were the exceptions, who in their moments of keenest despair would find their pot of gold.

Four miles from our cabin lived two men who had, like most of the others, become discouraged and ready to leave at the first

A gold mining operation on Bonanza Creek, circa 1899, near the claims purchased by William Knowles.

opportunity. We had not visited them for several weeks, when suddenly news came that they had struck a vein of gold and that their mine was immensely rich. Shortly after, we were at supper with them, hearing their excited talk of their good fortune. Gleefully they told of how they planned to go to the "Outside" on the first boat and fetch their families, and they bubbled all over with joy and anticipation.

But fortune had decided otherwise. The next day one of the partners set out for the hills to get wood. Having procured all that he could carry, he turned his dogs loose, for the trail was all downhill, and he could coast clear to his cabin. Down the trail he went, steering the sled with his gee pole. Approaching a sharp

Onlookers stand around a cart loaded with lumber that is mired in the mud in Dawson in 1898.

swerve in the path, he threw his whole weight against this guiding pole, and in so doing, placed his body in a direct line with the stump of a tree that had been chopped down in such a manner that some wooden prongs were left sticking out toward the trail. He was impaled upon one of these. His shrieks of agony brought men from nearby mines, but it was decided by his rescuers that he should be left in that position until a doctor could be brought from Dawson.

After hours of anguish, the doctor arrived, gave but temporary relief, and decided to take the man all the way to Dawson. In the hospital there, the wood was removed. The man wavered between life and death for several months, but finally recovered. When he returned to his mine, he found that his partner had filched him of his belongings and of any part of the title to the claim.

There were many such villains in the Klondike, made so by the insane greed for gold. Yet, there were also many men whose natures remained kind and generous in a country where it mattered little whether a man did bad or good, and where the incentives to do ill greatly over-balanced the incentives to do good.

The richest mine that I had seen was that worked by the Berry boys. Occasionally we would go to their claims for lunch, and then they would take us around to see their work. The cleaning room looked like the United States Mint. Their most valuable holdings came from the river bottom, where the gold was abundantly mixed with the sand. The shining metal was separated from the worthless dirt by the simple process of letting the mixed material drop from one pan to another and blowing the lighter, worthless sand away, so that only the gold fell to the pan. Whenever I looked around this room, I imagined I was looking at a million dollars in a glance.

In one corner were bags stacked up like cords of wood. Each contained about ten or twelve thousand dollars in gold dust. On the stoves were thousands of dollars in mixed dust drying, preparatory to the blowing process. In another corner there were buckets filled with nuggets, each stone being worth from one dollar to one hundred dollars. Was it no wonder that men were willing to battle any hardships for the possibility of gaining all this?

Clarence Berry took me to the riverbed where they mined this treasure. Pits had been dug down into the bed, where the dirt was removed in buckets. Clarence told me to climb down one of the ladders. I went down, examining the walls as I descended. In the very walls themselves I could see yellow streaks and nuggets!

"Pick out a nugget, Mrs. Knowles," Clarence instructed me, and I selected a small one.

"Now, I'll give you all you can wash in one pan," came another generous offer. The pan that I washed out was so heavy with gold that when weighed, it amounted to $375!

These men took millions out of this natural vault, and they were very reckless and generous with their wealth, as one might already have observed from the above. To everyone who was unfortunate and without work, these men always gave aid and employment; no disheartened creature was turned way from their mines. They had come to their wealth honestly and after months of tribulations in which they nearly froze and starved. Their generosity and kindness to everyone earned my respect and love. Could I ever forget their unselfishness in sending me the milk from their cow at the most critical time of my illness in Dawson?

And their kindness was extended to their dogs, as well as to human beings. When it was the expected thing to abuse the dogs, these influential men saw to it that no animal of theirs was ever maltreated. Just before Clarence left overland that winter, we sold Pete, our Indian dog, to him as a lead dog, for his had died. I could not bear to sell this affectionate and gentle animal to anyone else who probably would have begun by beating him up. Clarence apparently looked at these animals as I did, for he himself owned one, named Julian, which he treated like a human being, keeping it indoors at night and finally shipping it at great expense to the "Outside," where it spent its last days in Selma, California.

Prospecting for gold entailed many risks, and miners were seldom rewarded bounteously. One of the men who had first come in with my husband the year before, a man named Canfield, I believe, went on a prospecting trip one of these freezing days. He was with a party of several men. Following a lead his own, he became separated from his companions, and lost his way completely. His friends set out immediately in search of him, believing that he had matches and could build a fire to keep himself warm and to serve as a sort of distress signal. But the man apparently had no matches, or failed to start a fire with those he had, and as a result, wandered around for two days without food or fire, knowing that unless he happened upon some trail or other he would freeze to death.

His companions finally came to a place where a tree had been cut. Going farther on they found no trace of him, and after a consultation decided that he probably was buried under the snow near that tree. After digging around for a time, they finally found a piece of a shoe that had been chewed up, perhaps by the man himself. The snow was very deep, for it had been storming for several days now. Under a projecting rock, far down under the surface, they found him, still alive. They dared not build a fire, lest the sudden heat should kill him, so they carried him all the way to Dawson. The doctors there amputated his arms, legs, and nose. Becoming conscious, he saw the conditions he was in, and it was such a shock to him that he went suddenly insane. Months after, he regained his mind, but the misfortune was so terrible that he did not write to his folks at home, hoping that they supposed him dead. Several years later we learned from friends that he had died. I do not think that his people ever learned how he came to his death.

We were eating our lunch in our cramped cabin one day during the last part of May (we had been at the claims since February), when Willie suddenly startled us by pointing his finger and exclaiming: "Mama, mama! Look quick, and see the sun!"

We all looked toward where he was pointing, and there, above the door, streaming through a knothole, was a brilliant beam of light which shot its prismatic colors like a ribbon across the room. We all jumped up and ran out of the door. There was the sun, a great ball of grayish gold which sent its brown rays all over the sky and snow!

We all shouted like children who had for a long time been imprisoned in a dungeon, and for the first time had been liberated into the dazzling sunlight. It was joyous to bask in its light after having missed it for months. It peeked over the mountain at the south for only a half hour that day, but every day afterward it came up for a longer time. The weather became warm, and the snow quickly melted, leaving everything slushy at first, and then muddy.

My husband soon went down to Dawson to see if the river was ready "to go out," that is, to see if the ice was about to break up. Most of the miners were contemplating going down several days before the "going out," for this was the sight of the spring, and soon the boats would be coming up, bringing news, mail, and possibly friends. However, Will found that the trails were in very bad shape, and that a misstep often meant going down to his knee in mud. Everyone wore mutlock boots, made out of walrus skin, without any soles, and the frequent stepping on stones and gravel in the mud on the trail bruised the feet badly.

That evening he dragged himself in, with his feet badly swollen. When we had eased the pain, he told us his plans. He had been able to procure a cabin for us in Dawson, where we could spend the rest of the time before we left for the "Outside." This would give us a chance to see the river "go out," whenever it did, and we would be on hand to get the first news that came in from the outside world. As it would soon be sluicing time, and things would run smoothly at the mines, Will would only have to make one trip up each week. Glad for a change, and for a chance to see Dawson in the fast approaching summertime, we readily assented to his suggestions.

We began to pack up the next morning, and as our belongings were not colossal, it did not take us long. We had only one dog left now, Nig, for we had sold Pete and the other three some time before. Dogs can carry about seventy-five pounds in saddlebags, so we prepared a load for Nig. Besides this, we carried our own bedding and food. When the men heard that we were leaving immediately, they came in flocks to bid us adieu. They seemed to regret very much that little Willie was leaving because he had been a cheerful and sociable kid, and had had many good times with the lonely men.

At eight o'clock the following morning we departed. From the trail at the bottom of the hill I looked back at the cabin, standing up there with its door open. And despite its inconveniences, its crowdedness, its low rafters that always caught my hair, and its thousand other defects as a residence, the very fact that it had been "home" during all those frigid months made me want to turn back while there was yet time. The men who had been my close friends during my husband's illness were standing up there, waving to us until we would be out of sight. More than any of the rest of us, Willie did not want to leave. He had had a wonderful time during the winter, going from one cabin to another, and being every man's pet. Each of his best friends had given him a nugget, and as we had started down the hill, they had called after him, "Good-bye, old sport."

Our journey down resembled in no respect that of coming up. The sun had now come up to stay for more than twelve hours a day, and its warmth had brought a rich green bloom to the plants, which had for many months slept beneath the snow. All the trees and bushes were clothed in the richest verdure, but especially the rose bushes, which, though stunted by a harsh Mother Nature, now carried beautiful blossoms that perfumed the air. The moss on the banks and hills around us was fast losing its faded yellow garments, and wherever the sun had shone, it had become like green, feathery down. Strange flowers and plants that I had never before seen were growing up everywhere from out of the moss.

Though our journey was downhill, our packs were heavy and the gravel punched and hurt our feet terribly through our soft boots. Willie seemed to suffer most from the sharp gravel on his feet, but he bore it like a sport. We would carry him for a time, and when we stopped to rest, he would go to Nig, rest his head on the dog's fur, and go immediately to sleep.

Frequently we came to freshets, or larger streams, where our only bridges were logs that were small and not trustworthy. Our only accident occurred when Nig fell off of one of these logs. He pulled himself out of the water badly frightened and looking as sheepish as if someone had purposely abused him.

Just before sunset we came to a place where we had to cross the Klondike River. My heart almost stopped beating when I saw how we had to cross that raging, plunging current! Had I known that we would have to cross that dangerous torrent, I would never have come. One long log stretched half way across to a pile of rocks in the middle of the stream. Then another log went across to the bank beyond. A hundred feet below us, the water was dashing against huge boulders and making a frightful noise.

I watched my husband carry all the luggage over, treading on the log, which had been smoothed on top, with confidence and calmness. Then he took Willie, who was not at all enthusiastic about the excursion, and tucking him tightly under his arm, cautioning him not to make a move, he walked across again. The little fellow seemed skeptically brave, saying over and over, "Papa, don't let me fall!" Nig, the dog, saw that his turn was next, and coming over to me, lay down at my feet. My husband urged the dog again and again to go across, but the frightened dog looked up at me in a sort of pleading, trusting way, as if to say, "Don't let him make me go over." Afraid that continued urging would cause him to flee back to our cabin, we soon left off coaxing him. By this time, having seen my husband go across so many times, I decided that I could do it myself. I had my husband walk in front of me while we both counted, "one-two, one-two," beginning before we started on the log. As we slowly went across, I was too frightened to look down at the swift water beneath my feet. After what seemed like ages, we reached the opposite bank, where I felt so weak that I almost sank down. Looking back, I saw Nig hesitate, and then, making up his mind, he came across at a run. When he reached us, he jumped up and licked my face before I could ward him off! This certainly indicated to me that a dog, at least this dog, knows and understands considerably more than it is given credit for.

The excitement of this crossing swept away every feeling of tiredness. We had yet the most dangerous section of the river to cross, but this part was crossed in a boat pulled by a cable wire, and another tributary was crossed in a boat that was rowed. On the bank of this last stream was the log hotel at which we had planned to spend the night. This hostelry was filled with men loudly talking and laughing, and I knew that with this distraction and the noise of the raging river, which almost swept under the hotel itself, I would not be able to sleep that night. After a dinner of pork and beans, hot bread, dried apples, potatoes and coffee, we felt so refreshed that we decided to go on to Dawson.

The surprising thing was that the sun was still up, and would not set until past eleven. As we sauntered along in the cool and crisp evening, the air was very refreshing, and it seemed that all nature was bursting with life. Occasionally we came to patches of ice that we could see through, and down beneath those transparent beds, one could see plants and even flowers growing, apparently all snug and warm.

Just before we reached Dawson, we came to the cabin of a friend of my husband's, who was so homesick that he would not permit us to go on until he had prepared a second supper for us. This man kept himself next to starvation by his large heart, which never permitted him to turn away anybody who came to him in need. His home was that of a typical Dawson bachelor: cooking utensils and wearing apparel piled together in one corner, a few boxes to sit on, a pole bed, a table, and a stove—that was all. The floor was hard, cold ground, as smooth as glass. He had been here two years, working a claim that had been misrepresented to him—a claim that he had sold all of his property in the States to purchase. Now he was in poverty, and planned to go out on the first boat that went. He was old and broken, and had no prospects. This man walked with us until we saw the lights of Dawson, and then we left him—a sad figure standing there on the trail—disillusioned.

We found our cabin located on the hill behind the center of town. When we opened the door, we found the floor wholly covered with water, and though exhausted, we swept it out, started the fire, and were soon asleep in the pole beds. We found difficulty in sleeping because of the light that streamed in through the window. Unable to adjust ourselves to this perpetual daylight, we tacked a piece of canvas over the window to suggest nighttime to us.

We were almost asleep when we were jerked out of our beds by a terrific din just outside our door. It sounded as if a thousand dogs were barking and fighting there. My husband grabbed a stick of wood and rushed to the door. He was met by two thin and hungry malamutes who, when they saw him, were so frightened that they howled and ran down the hill. They had smelled our supper and would have robbed our larder could they have reached it. These were only two of the large army of dogs that had been turned loose by mushers when they could not be of use any longer as freight pullers. It was costly to feed these dogs, and carrying them over from winter to winter was considerably more expensive than buying new animals at the beginning of the snows. Hence the poor animals were left to a death of slow starvation. Some of the dogs managed to eke out an existence on the filth of the town, and it was even noised about that they frequented the graveyards, where the graves were shallow. Though this repulsive notion was scoffed at by many, I myself heard dogs howling up in the cemetery, which was not far from our cabin.

After my husband returned the next night from carrying the remainder of our belongings down from the claims, I was startled by his thin and worn appearance. He had so wanted to make good here, so that we would have money when we went home, that he had worked and worried night and day for many months, and I was afraid that he would break down with fatigue. I decided then that we would all start for the "Outside," if possible on the first boat.

The warm days of the Alaskan summer became longer and longer, and soon it was light all day and most of the night. All measure of time, besides looking at the clock, disappeared. One day when my husband had not returned from the mines as soon as I expected, Willie and I went for a long walk, and then sat out in our yard in the sun, I sewing and Willie playing with the dog.

After a while I became a little sleepy and had just decided to go to bed, expecting that perhaps my husband would return the next day, when he suddenly appeared. He immediately asked why we had stayed up so late for him. I had not thought it late, but when I looked at my watch, I found that it was three o'clock in the morning! One could now read or sew all night, for the sun was only out of sight for two hours.

The days became quite uninteresting, being long and unvarying. One morning Willie and I went through the town and down to the river, where we saw a musher beating his dogs, cracking his whip over their heads, and swearing obscenely. The animals were paralyzed with fright. I grabbed Willie by the hand and hastened back to our cabin. I was fully determined not to go into the town again except when necessary, and to leave this land of brutality as soon as possible.

The breaking up and "going out" of the ice into the river occurred one Sunday. The whole of Dawson and most of the men in the mining camps for miles around were on hand to see this momentous phenomenon. The great mass of ice began slowly to move on the surface of the swollen river, and here and there it would pile up into huge mountains of crystal blocks. Then the water would "pile up" behind these masses and suddenly the whole mound would give way with a great roar, the tumbling of ice and the rushing of the water filling the air with loud claps of thunder and shaking the ground. Sometimes the water would back up and overflow the banks, carrying away tents and debris. The people all around were greatly impressed and excited by the sight, and I frequently listened to tales of how the town of Dawson had been wiped out by the river in previous years when the ice had broken up.

The Klondike River at our left was now a raging, destructive torrent of water, and where it plunged into the Yukon, it rose to the very tops of the bank and threatened to sweep over it. The water foamed and frothed where these two great rivers rushed together, and what with the swish of the water and the grinding of the ice, which could be heard for miles, the scene was very startling. Finally, as we watched, we saw the last jam break down, and the ice cakes go sailing down the river toward the ocean. The Yukon was clear! Now boats would be coming up, and would bring letters and news of my little girls, whom I had not heard from for ten long months. Now the river was clear and the "Outside"—home—did not seem so far away.

The Hazardous Voyage Home

With the Yukon now open to the "Outside," our whole aspect of life changed. It seemed as if everyone in Dawson suddenly changed from a sullen, gloomy person to a happy, relieved and hopeful one. The first boats began to arrive, and it was joyous to hear the shouts of welcome that received them. When a boat would land and someone on board would call, "Hello, John," I saw big men weep with joy at seeing and hearing their friends.

Watching the first boat going out was another of the sights of the season, and everyone was present, prepared to see the fortunate ones leaving. "Baby Dawson," the first white baby born in Dawson, was going out on the first boat. She was the mascot of the whole town, especially as her birth was accompanied by the most sorrowful events. Her mother, who had come in at the same time we had, had left her home in Ohio as a bride to go with her husband to the Klondike. At her departure, her father, a sentimental old fellow, had taken an American flag, wrapped it around her, and said: "My daughter, this flag will protect you wherever you may go or wherever you may live; take it, and God bless you." These same words had been repeated over her dead body in Dawson, with the flag wrapped about her as a shroud, and with the last boat waiting to carry her remains back to her father. The mother had died at childbirth and the firstborn of Dawson remained at her birthplace, because it was thought best not to subject it to the rigors of a precarious ocean voyage.

The baby had been well kept, and was one of the main attractions of the town. Many of the men from the mines came to visit her and to fondle the babe, each one feeling that he had a certain personal responsibility to this little northerner. Now the banks of the river were crowded with those who had come to bid the child good-bye. As the boat began to move away, nuggets, watches, and other pieces of jewelry were tossed to her. As far as we could see, the baby continued to laugh and clap its hands.

The thawing out of the ground brought one wonderful thing—the growing of fresh vegetables! Many people had long been suffering from scurvy, and the only hope for relief rested in the shipment of green things on the first boats, and the growing of vegetables here. The summers were not more than two months long, hardly enough time for the ground to thaw out, but I saw some fine vegetables growing before I left. I remember that my husband at one time went down to Dawson, where in one of the stores he had spied some potatoes. He bought three at a dollar apiece. Though they were miserable specimens, when we saw them lying steaming on our table, we looked at them as if they were diamonds. But when we ate them, peels and all, we found them sunburned and tasteless. Our own dried potatoes tasted better.

Summer was now passing swiftly and as yet I had heard nothing about leaving. Then my husband came in one day with a broad smile on his face, picked up Willie, danced around the room with him, and then grabbed me around the waist and gave me a whirl or two. I thought that a letter had perhaps come, for several boats had arrived. But the surprise and joy was greater. He told how he had just received my ticket for the boat going to San Francisco the next Saturday, only a few days off! We screamed with joy and I grabbed and squeezed Willie and my husband in turns. The child and the dog scampered around the room. Suddenly I noticed that my husband had not entered into our ecstasy—and then I realized that he had said *my* ticket and not *our* tickets. All of my pleasure died instantly. Our clamor of questions resulted in Will telling us that the men who had intended to purchase our claims had suddenly "backed out," and that he could not go home, perhaps not until after the last boat had left for the "Outside," in which case he would have to go out overland.

There could have been no greater disappointment. After all of our rapturous planning about how we would sail down the Yukon together toward home, leaving only memories behind us, then came this calamity! A whole month ahead of time and unknown to me, my husband had reserved our tickets, not suspecting that his plan would be thus upset. His plan had been that we should go out via the ocean, for we could then rest and have nourishing food.

I flatly refused to go without him, telling him to go down and sell my ticket, just as he had already sold his. Tickets had to be reserved a long time ahead, and I knew that many would buy my ticket immediately for a larger sum than that which we paid for it. But my husband was determined that we should go out while we had a chance. If we waited, we might not even be able to go out on the last boat, and then the only way out would have been overland, a trip that he considered too difficult for us.

I made no move to pack, hoping that something would turn up, and that he would be able to go with us. Secretly I was sorry that I had shown so much elation over going when he first told us. Afterwards he told me that he had been considering at first selling our ticket also, but when he saw our rejoicing, he realized how utterly homesick we were. This definitely convinced him that Willie and I should go.

The next few days I said nothing about the trip and cautioned Willie to be mum, too, hoping that after further consideration my husband would let us stay with him.

"What are you going to wear on the boat?" he suddenly asked me on Friday night, just a night before the steamer left. I immediately exclaimed that I would not go a step without him, and that nothing more need be said about the trip. But he thought otherwise, and the dispute that followed showed me that arguing was useless. We were to go while we had the chance.

As far as clothes and personal belongings were concerned, we were ready to leave at a moment's notice. The most presentable garments I had to wear were a short dress, moccasins, a fur cap, and my "parkie." Everything I had of a "dressy" nature I had sold after the trip in: my hat and gloves were sold to an Indian woman, and my best dress went for an enormous price.

We could not sleep that night; the anticipation of the separation was too heavy a thought. My nephew, Charlie, had come in from the mines to see us off, and we all visited far into the night, going over our experiences and our plans. Charlie planned to stay on until he had made a big enough "stake" to purchase a farm in California. Willie was excited and could not sleep well either. He would occasionally wake up and talk about going home to see his sisters.

We ate our breakfast at three o'clock in the morning, with the sun shining through the window. Our poor dog, Nig, seemed to understand perfectly well what all the commotion was about. He would eat no breakfast. He kept following me all over the cabin, finally getting in the way so much that we had to chain him outside. I felt badly to think that I could not take him with me, the boat company refusing to let the dog aboard. I had long contemplated taking this most human affectionate dog with me to the "Outside." My husband said that if possible he would bring the animal out with him.

At nine o'clock we started for the boat, Charlie carrying my basket on his head, my husband with Willie on his back, and I following. When I left the cabin, there was Nig chained to the tree, whining. I went to him, took his head in my lap, and could not help but weep. The animal seemed to understand that I was not going to take him with me. When I got up, he gave the most human moan, watching in a pleading way every little movement I made. Feeling almost as if I were leaving one of my own children, I ran down the hill. Even when I reached the bank of the river, I could hear him wailing away back there at the cabin, and I felt distinctly unhappy.

After the good-byes were said, the boat pulled away from shore. It was a very difficult *au-revoir*, and I would have given anything had I been able to go back to Will and stay until he left. Underneath his forced smile, I could see that he was dejected and sadly disappointed at not going with his wife and child. Just for a moment the steamer, a very large one, stopped in mid-stream, and thinking that it was going to go back for something, I planned to jump off of it and refuse to go on. There were men on shore who would have bought my ticket instantly and would have paid a large sum for it. But bad luck! We started again, and soon were slipping down the river.

As I stood there on the back of the boat watching Dawson slowly fade in the distance, in those moments I thought of the anxious days we had spent in our little boat going through all of those dangers and hardships on the Upper Yukon in our efforts to reach Dawson before the winter came onto us. I thought of how, a year before, we looked at the twinkling lights of this town for the first time, as if it were the final haven of rest, and now I was going away wiser. Yet, despite its brutality, its crudity, its disease, its defects, how could I help looking back at those humble cabins and shacks in Dawson without thinking of all the warm friends among the miners, and of those whose lot was too hard to bear in temperance? All the diseases and other troubles had knitted us into one large family.

A motley assembly it was on this boat, many of whom were my friends. There were three hundred miners, eight women, and two children on board. Many of them were sick, with no one to attend them. All had to shift for themselves, for there was no doctor or steward on board.

The trip downstream had many beauties, for the land all around us was green, flowery, and cheerful. We stopped every day to take on wood for the engines, and at those times all the passengers who were able landed and went for strolls into the surrounding country. One such time, I saw a man wander away and not return at the time the boat whistled for departure. I ran to the captain and told him of the belated passenger. The whistle was blown and blown, and finally the man came running up, red-faced and out of breath; he had found a strange and wonderful flower which no one had ever seen before. He gave it to me for holding the boat. Examining it, I was amazed to find that in many details it looked like a little cradle made of wax, supporting a little baby on its down bed. The leaves around it were red, the stem a vivid green. Several days later, on going to my stateroom, I found that someone had entered and had stolen this gorgeous plant.

We were a day before Circle City and traveling swiftly when we all heard a call of help coming from the land. The snow was still on the ground here and for some distance back to the mountains in this desolate country, where there were no trees or shrubs. We slowed up, and soon saw several men standing on the bank, waving their hands and shouting. What looked like a stretcher with a body on it was lying at their feet. We drew to the shore, and took aboard these men and their burden. We all stood around wide-eyed as they told their story.

These two men, who had been out prospecting about forty miles from Circle City, had wandered onto a tent that seemed to be ready to fall down. Inside they had heard someone moaning. Entering, they discovered a man who seemed to be nearer death than life, and was in a badly starved condition. Some warmed canned milk revived him sufficiently so that he told his story.

It seemed that he and his brother had been prospecting in these strange mountains when a terrible storm came up, which prevented their traveling. This man became very ill and unable to travel, so his brother started out for Dawson to get food and help. That had been *two months* before! Probably the brother had died on the way, for no one had come to succor this man, who continued so weak from his sickness that he could not build a fire or cook. He had managed to keep life in himself all this time by eating dried beans and dried fish. His dog starved to death in the tent with him. From eating this dry food he was continually thirsty, and the snow which he could reach did not satisfy him. Around him at night he could hear wild animals prowling, and he expected death at any time. He would lapse into states of unconsciousness at times, and then be revived, but at no time was he strong enough to move. He was unable to bury the dog, therefore, or even to drag it outside, and the stench from the dead animal was nearly suffocating.

It was long after he had given up hope that the men found him. His rescuers made a stretcher out of a blanket, and headed for the river, hoping to be picked up by some steamer. The journey to the river had been very long. The weather had turned cold, the country was very rough, and their food had run out. Consequently, when we picked them up, they were nearly starved themselves.

When we came to Circle City, these Good Samaritans got off. After we got started down the river again, I went in to visit and to encourage the man who had suffered such privation. The poor fellow was not only ill but very much depressed at the thought that he did not have enough money to pay for a ticket even to St. Michael, where we changed to an ocean-going steamer. I left him and in a short time had taken up a collection from the passengers which enabled him to pay for a passage clear to San Francisco. He was completely overcome when the money was placed in his hands.

About half the way to the mouth of the Yukon there was a Catholic mission where we were to stop to take on some passengers and wood. The Indians there came out to meet us in their birch canoes, but when we turned towards them on our way to the shore, they were so frightened by the immensity of our boat that they jumped out of their canoes into the water, and putting the canoes over their heads, they swam swiftly to shore. These canoes were so light, being made out of birch bark and skins, that a child could lift them. One old woman tried to turn around so quickly that she and her basket of goods, which she had planned to sell, went overboard. I thought she had drowned, it took her so long to come up, but later found that she had lost her money bag and was swimming around underneath trying to get it.

We went ashore here and examined the Eskimo village. The Indians did not like for us to intrude into their camps: the women went into their tepees, closing the doorways when they saw us coming, and the little children timidly hid their faces and ran away when we tried to talk to them. The priests here were very much beloved by the Indians because of their unselfish devotion and courage in helping the natives in all of their distresses. I was told that diseases were fast taking these people off, and that they would probably be extinct in another generation. The Eskimos themselves looked very happy and content. For food and fuel (whale blubber) they went down to the ocean at the mouth of the river, where sperm whales lived in great schools. These were the people who in wintertime dig a hole in the snow and then build a round dome or room out of the ice and snow. The fire is built in the center of this room, where they do their cooking and eating, and toward which they point their feet when they sleep.

Before we reached the mouth of the river, we entered the zone where one could see the sun for twenty-four hours of the day, and where in winter there is nothing but blackness for months. At the mouth of the Yukon the river is full of treacherous sand bars and islands, but we had an Indian pilot aboard who knew how to avoid the shoals. The river divides into several mouths where it debouches into the sea, and here to the horizon on every side, one sees only water and islands which are covered with low trees and brush. Before we entered the ocean proper, we came upon an incoming steamer which had been stuck fast on a bar. We came in close, threw ropes to the helpless boat, and after several attempts finally pulled it into deep water. We also saw several stranded boats which had been abandoned.

Leaving the mouth we traveled north toward St. Michael. The bay at which this trading post was located was very rough when we arrived, and our river boat had difficulty in making a landing. Our ocean steamer, the *Bertha*, was laying there, the ship which was to take us to San Francisco. The town of St. Michael was a small place holding only several stores, a few log cabins, and a church. When I looked over the *Bertha* lying there at the wharf, any elation which I might have held regarding the trip from this point to California disappeared. The steamer looked small and unstable, and was, in fact, the smallest boat making this long ocean trip. The fact that there was a hard storm threatening did not improve my spirits.

When we boarded and hunted for our berth, the captain informed me that he had none for me and Willie. Despite the fact that I told him my husband had reserved a place for us a month before, he told me that I would have to stay in St. Michael until the next boat went. The company, he said, would pay all my expenses. Just as I was ready to get off, a stranger came up, told the captain that he could give his state room to me, and wait himself for the next boat. I did not get to see this man, and he did not even wait to be thanked. Here was just another of those many acts of kindness which I had seen miners show to people in distress.

On this ship there was neither a doctor nor steward, and the bunks were filled with sick, helpless people. The boat had a frightful time getting out of the bay, for the storm was now raging out on the ocean. The terrifying thing to me was that the captain admitted that our boat did not have ballast, a violation of the law itself, and an exceedingly dangerous thing for us in the rough weather; our little craft bobbed and plunged about in the water in such an uncontrolled way that I was sure that we would go to the bottom before the next morning. The night was appalling, as we bounced around on those huge breakers, especially since we had so many sick people on board. The captain himself said that if the storm did not let up before morning we would have to turn back to St. Michael. Happily, after several exciting hours the storm did not rage so furiously. Later we learned that in this same storm five of the largest steamers going north from San Francisco were lost.[9] The only thing that saved us, I guess, was that we were on the edge of it.

For three days we were among the whales. These animals, who seemed not at all afraid of the boat, but in fact interested in it, would swim all around us blowing water from their snouts high up in the air. They tumbled and played with each other like kittens, and seemed especially fond of diving under our boat. They were so huge and looked so strong that whenever they would dive under us, everyone would hold his breath in excitement, fearing that they would bump us over.

9. Although there were various shipwrecks involving steamships during those years, it's not clear to which ships she was referring.

When we were hundreds of miles from shore, it seemed, we saw birds as large as geese flying around us. They could not fly very fast, for their wings were small and looked as if they had been trimmed. Some of the men baited a line and caught some of these gray and brown-colored birds. When we placed them on the deck, the awkward creatures could hardly walk, and after a few moments they seemed to get seasick. We could then handle them, place them on their backs with feet up, or put them in any position we wanted, and they would not move. The captain said that he always saved the garbage for this place, where the birds were always waiting for him.

At another place we ran through a school of fish that looked as if they had miniature sails which carried them along on top of the water. We lowered a bucket, brought some on deck, and studied their movements. Whenever we touched their sails, they immediately drew them down onto their backs.

Gambling and drinking went on for days and nights in the saloon. The men would sit around the tables, which were heaped with thousands of dollars in gold dust, saying no word for hours as the money changed hands. Some men lost thousands; one whom I knew personally lost his entire fortune which he had taken two years to mine in Dawson, and with which he had planned to buy a home for the family in the states. I felt that the men with whom he was playing should not have let him gamble his money away when he was drunk and irresponsible. He had to borrow money before he could get off the boat when we landed at San Francisco.

The trip was very hard. There were no comforts and the food was poor. Our journey should have taken eighteen days but we were already a week late because of the numerous and terrific storms that assailed us continually on the way. Practically all of the passengers were sick now; and with no doctor or stewardess to help them, the poor captain was called out at all times of the night and day to minister unto someone who thought he was dying. Fortunately I did not get sick myself, and was able to go around and help some of those that needed attention. There were no fresh vegetables aboard, and sufferers from scurvy were numerous.

One girl, only nineteen, who had been operated upon in Dawson for appendicitis, seemed to me dangerously ill. This young thing had led an immoral life in Dawson, but I found her to be a tender, kind-hearted creature. One morning she told me that she felt that she was going to get well. I asked her what she would have for breakfast. With a wistful look on her face, she said that she would almost give her life for something good to eat. Now, it had happened that one day I had passed the kitchen just as the cook was taking something out of the refrigerator, and laying in that cool chamber I had seen several large pieces of beef. As this girl, whose strength was rapidly waning on the poor fare of the ship, now almost pleaded for some real food, I made up the mind.

"Captain," I said a minute later, "I want some fresh meat for Miss ----."

"Sorry, Mrs. Knowles," he replied, "there is not a bit on the ship. How can you expect..."

"Not very long ago, I saw some fresh beef in the cook's refrigerator, and I must have some of it immediately for this sick girl. You know, of course, that if this woman dies on the trip, you can be condemned for sailing without a doctor for all of these ill people."

I was in the kitchen in a few minutes, myself cooking a nice piece of this fresh flesh for the girl, for I wanted to retain all of its juices and if possible invigorate her. The captain had been a little

The steamer Roanoke *arriving in Seattle with gold miners returning from the Klondike on July 19, 1898.*

frightened, and was ready to do anything to keep from having to turn back to the Unger Islands in Alaska to get a doctor for her. This would have meant a two weeks' delay. When the poor girl saw the princely breakfast, tears filled her eyes in gratitude, not so much for the meat but for the fact that someone had respected her enough to go to any pains over her wellbeing.

The officers of the ship seemed to be getting liquor surreptitiously. This annoyed the captain, who was unable to discover who was giving it to them. There were several rich miners aboard who had smuggled liquor with them, and were giving draughts to the officers and the help of the boat on the sly. Finally at the dinner table one evening, the captain announced that if the person who was getting the men drunk did not desist, he would be forced to search every stateroom for the whiskey, and would place the guilty person or persons in the hands of the law. After this there was no more trouble, and there was no longer any danger of our journey miscarrying.

As we approached San Francisco, the demeanor of everyone changed. We would soon be home! The water was now perfectly calm, and we would sit out on the decks in the evenings feeling warm and happy. The gambling and drinking had ceased now that we were only a day out of San Francisco, most everyone collecting on the deck in excited anticipation. The night before entering the Golden Gate, the men walked and talked on the deck all night. Some had been in Dawson for several years and were taking out small fortunes. Others were broken in body and spirit, owing money for the very passage out of that dismal land.

At six the next morning everyone was at the rail straining his eyes to catch the first glimpse of the great city. There was no fog, the water was smooth, and everyone happy. Suddenly there came the shout of discovery, and in a moment we all saw the Golden Gate down on the horizon. As we rapidly approached it, we all chattered happily, mainly about one thing—what we were going to eat when we landed. Even the invalids, who had found strength to come on deck, were joking and laughing, some almost to the point of hysteria. As we were passing through the Gate, small boats filled with reporters flocked to meet us, to find out why we had been so late in coming, to see, perhaps, why we had not drowned.

Nearing the wharf we entered a small fleet of little boats holding over-anxious friends and relatives who wanted to see as soon as possible if some loved one was safe on board. There was a great babel of voices, those of the welcomers in the boats shouting to people on board, and throwing fruit to them, and those of us on the ship who shrieked with joy, throwing handkerchiefs, hats, and anything handy up into the air in our excitement. Some of the men I thought would jump overboard when they saw wives and mothers.

San Francisco filled us long imprisoned ones full of awe and wonder, and we could hardly wait to land, to put our feet once more on civilized soil. The dock was loaded with people. I saw two women faint as their loved ones were carried off in stretchers. The noise and confusion on the dock was deafening. Hacks from the hotels lined the dock, and the yelling of the drivers sounded not so different from the howls of the malamutes. To me this clash of noise was new and disagreeable, and I caught myself wishing a little that I were back in the quiet north, where it was only the sound of the steady picking of pick-axes, the distant murmur of mushers urging their dogs and cracking their whips, and the musical swish of the sleds from side to side on the trail, that broke the stillness.

I had no one to meet me for I had written my family early that I would be home on the last boat from Dawson. Like everyone else, Willie and I went up town immediately, feeling of course conspicuous in our northern furs and moccasins. There I telegraphed to my little girls and their aunt when I would arrive in Capitola, where they were staying. After buying my girls a few presents, I went to South San Francisco, to the home of the wife of one of the miners, named Museau, who had given me a money belt to carry to his family.

We were ravenously hungry for civilized food, but appeased our appetites a little by munching some delicious fruit on the way. Mrs. Museau welcomed us gladly. While telling her about her husband, Willie and I smelled some dumplings which were cooking in the next room, and were beside ourselves with the desire to rush out and help ourselves. But we were not invited to eat any—of course this woman did not know our desire—and we went away feeling almost ill with hunger.

It was the evening train that brought us to Capitola, where my daughters were waiting to greet us. To the mother's eye that had not seen them for a full year, they had grown and changed much. I felt as if I had been buried for years. Their happiness was marred by the absence of their father, and they felt badly to think that they would not see him for several months.

To be near my husband's sister until he should come out of the north, I rented a cabin in Capitola. The next morning after my arrival, we moved into our little home. We were a happy family that day as we got our things in order, the little girls listening with open eyes to Willie and I as we told of the wondrous things of the far north. For a whole year we had been separated, and here we were now despite our hardships all safely together again—except for the children's father.

When night came we all sat around the table talking, talking of the land of gold. A gentle rap came at the door. Little Hazel ran to the door, pulled it open, and then gave a scream of joy. I looked up, and there stood my husband holding the girl in his arms! Yes, my eyes were telling me right: there stood the children's father, dressed in his northern furs, smothered by the welcome of the children. No surprise could have been greater!

As soon as we could compose ourselves, he told us his good fortune. Immediately after Willie and I had steamed away from Dawson, he had gone up into the town, and had run into a man who offered to purchase the mines outright. In a week the papers had been signed, and my husband was on his way overland, having been invited by friends to join a party coming this shorter way to the "Outside." He had hoped to reach San Francisco about the same time as I did, and had missed it by only two days.

What a joyous reunion was the one that night in the little cabin in Capitola, with our children all about us, healthy and happy! What a contrast to the year before, when the prospects for the coming year were gloomy and dangerous! This year had brought us much: though we had come back from the North not rich in gold, we were rich in a greater thing perhaps—experience! We had seen people like us fighting under galling handicaps, and had discerned under many crude and rough exteriors kind-heartedness, and good intentions.

FINIS

Appendix

Article in the *Oakland Tribune*, Dec. 30, 1897 (page 8):

MARVELOUS OUTPUT OF CLONDYKE GOLD
W.E. Knowles Purchases a Rich Claim
for Thousands of Dollars

"W.E. Knowles, who is a member of the real estate firm of Samuel & Knowles claims to have made a rich strike on Bonanza Creek in the Clondyke district. In partnership with Frank Berry, brother of Clarence Berry, the Clondyke King, he bought a claim for $250,000 in cash. Knowles says there is $1,000,000 in sight and the men who are working it have plenty of food and supplies and

this is the claim from which $24,000 was taken out last year from eight box lengths. The pay streak is 100 feet wide and 12 men are employed to take out the gold. The men who formerly owned the mine are R.E. and G.T. Edgar of Fresno, Cal.; P. I. McDonald, J.A. Williams and J.C. Felix.

Knowles and Berry also purchased claim No. 17 on Gold Bottom Creek. This property is reported to have prospected well and to be in close proximity to another prospect, which yields as high as $5 and $6 to the pan.

Knowles returned from Alaska on the steamer Al-Ki. He says that, although provisions are scarce, there is no danger of starvation on the Clondyke. He estimates the winter gold output at $12,000,000."

Biography of Josephine Knowles

Josephine Skelton was born on July 22, 1864, in Buffalo Prairie, Illinois. She lived in Nebraska and later California, where she married William E. Knowles. They had three children: Rose, Hazel, and William.

In 1898, Josephine and her husband traveled to the Klondike together with their three-year-old son and their nephew Charlie. They returned to California the following year in 1899, and lived the rest of their lives in Berkeley.

Josephine's husband died in 1913. She died in 1936 at the age of 71.

Her book about her experiences in the Klondike might have been lost if her granddaughter Muriel James had not found the manuscript and decided to finally have it published.

Sources of Photographs

Alaska State Library, Historical Collections. Juneau, Alaska.

The Huntington Library, Jack London
Papers. San Marino, California.

Museum of History & Industry (MOHAI),
Anders B. Wilse Collection. Seattle.

University of Washington Libraries, Special Collections.

Family photographs of Josephine and William Knowles.

Index

Gold Rush in the Klondike

stop at Bennett, 44–48
stop at Fort Selkirk, 69–71
stop at Forty Mile, 74–77
stop at Lake Lindeman, 26–34
stop at Sheep Camp, 20–21
Knowles, William "Willie" Jr. (son), 10, 42
cabin at Louse Town, 79–95
climbing Chilkoot Pass, 22–24
dogs and, 50, 79
move from Dawson to mines, 122–125
move to Dawson from mines, 141–147
navigating the Yukon River, 71–74
navigating White Horse Rapids, 60–65
relationship with men at mines, 95, 123, 129, 141
return to San Francisco, 150–165
stop at Lake Bennett, 44–48
stop at Bennett, 44–48
stop at Fort Selkirk, 69–71
stop at Forty Mile, 74–77
stop at Lake Lindeman, 26–34
stop at Sheep Camp, 20–21
trip to Dawson, 10–95

Lake Bennett, 24, 35, 46–48
crossing, 36–40
Lake Lebarge, 67, 71
Lake Lindeman, 5–6, 22, 24–25, 44, 67
camp, 29–33, 42
hotel, 26–28
trail to, 36–40
London, Jack, 15–16, 31–32
Louse Town, 77–95
cabin, 79–82, 109
winter, 86–110
women in, 115–118

the Mascot, 16
Monte Cristo mine, 88, 91
Museau (Mrs.), 164–165

the Narrows, 11
The New York Times, 93
Northern lights, 65–66, 133–134
Northwest Trading and Commission Co., 83

Oakland Mole, 5
Oakland Tribune, 7
One Mile River, 67

Parkies, 104–105, 121, 151
Pioneer Bakery and Café, 83

Queen, 10

St. George (Mr.), 123–125, 129–130, 132
St. Michael, 155, 157–158
Salvation Army, 115, 118
San Francisco, 162–165
The Scales, 7, 20
Seattle, WA, 10–11
Sheep Camp, 5, 16–20
hotel, 18–19
Skagway, 13–14
harbor, 12
Indian graves at, 12

Tagish Lake, 52
Treadwell mines, 12

Unger Islands, 161

White Horse Rapids, 50, 56, 60–65
White Pass Trail, 46
Windy Arm, 50–52

Yukon River, 11, 20, 24, 71–74, 83
Catholic mission, 155–156
winter, 84–86
Yukon Trail, 15

172